The
Golden Age
— of —
BICYCLE
RACING
in
NEW JERSEY

---·•·---

MICHAEL C. GABRIELE

Foreword by

PETER J. NYE

Charleston   London

THE
History
PRESS

Published by The History Press
Charleston, SC 29403
www.historypress.net

Front and back cover images: *Courtesy of Joseph M. Laufer, H.B. Smith Industrial Village Conservancy; the Newark Public Library; Jeff Groman, Jazz Sport LLC; and Peter J. Rutledge and George Coates Sr.*

First published 2011

Manufactured in the United States

ISBN 978.1.59629.427.1

Library of Congress Cataloging-in-Publication Data

Gabriele, Michael C.
The golden age of bicycle racing in New Jersey / Michael C. Gabriele ; foreword by Peter J. Nye.
p. cm.
Includes bibliographical references.
ISBN 978-1-59629-427-1
1. Bicycle racing--New Jersey--History. I. Title.
GV1045.5.N5G34 2011
796.6'2009749--dc22
2010053828

Broken bicycles, old busted chains
With rusted handle bars, out in the rain
Somebody must have an orphanage for
All these things that nobody wants any more
September's reminding July
It's time to be saying goodbye
Summer is gone, but our love will remain
Like old broken bicycles, out in the rain
—*"Broken Bicycles" by Tom Waits. Soundtrack song from the 1982*
movie One from the Heart

CONTENTS

CONTENTS

Foreword

BICYCLE RACING:
NEW JERSEY'S NATIONAL SPORT

By Peter Joffre Nye

Newark, Nutley and Somerville.
 For more than a century, these New Jersey venues have served as destinations for generations of the best bicycle racers from around the United States and Canada, Europe, Australia and New Zealand. Newark and Nutley were renowned for their outdoor board cycling tracks, called velodromes, in the 1890s through the 1930s, while Somerville, since 1940, has hosted a program of annual circuit races around its downtown every Memorial Day. Winners of events in all three Garden State towns make up international bicycle racing's Who's Who.

Alf Goullet grew up on a farm outside of Sydney, Australia, and arrived in 1910 in Newark when he was nineteen, determined to test himself against the greatest talents of his day. "I heard about Newark in Australia because of its velodrome," he recalled in the 1980s. "Our best riders went to Newark to race and came back with stories about New Jersey. They said if I felt I was really good, I had to go to Newark and measure myself against the best in the world."

He and others dazzled the 12,500 spectators who filled the grandstand on the finishing straight and the bleachers that surrounded the velodrome, six laps to the mile. From May through September, crowds flocked to watch programs held twice a week. Only when tickets sold out, the overflow beat a path to Wiedenmayer Park to watch the Class A Newark Bears play baseball.

View of back wall of Newark Velodrome grandstands. *Courtesy of Jeff Groman, Jazz Sport LLC.*

When Goullet immigrated, bicycle racers were among America's best-paid athletes. He soon earned $20,000 and more each year, from prize money and appearance fees, when Ty Cobb of the Detroit Tigers won American League batting championships on a salary of a mere $10,000.

Newark hosted the 1912 world championships. They culminated in the professional sprint contest. The one-mile final came down to a three-rider contest: Frank Kramer of East Orange, New Jersey, against national champions from Tasmania and France. Kramer won. He ruled as the fastest cyclist in the world.

Kramer, nearly six feet but appearing taller because he stood as straight as a water tower, turned into such a hero, he advertised Cadillacs. National ads depicted Kramer on his bicycle with this teaser: "Frank Kramer drives a Cadillac. Why don't you?"

Many foreign cyclists like Goullet became U.S. citizens and settled in New Jersey to raise families. Those top riders inspired successive generations, who grew up watching the giants of the sport compete. Among them was Bill Honeman of Newark, who turned pro at nineteen in 1928. He made his debut against French sprinter Pierre Guyot. Honeman, coached by Kramer, won decisively and started to follow Kramer's wheelmarks.

Bicycle Racing: New Jersey's National Sport

In September 1930, however, American cycling began a sharp dive. The lease on the grounds of the Newark Velodrome ran out, and the track was demolished, following the demise of tracks in other cities. Yet Honeman had acquired a golden reputation that earned him invitations to compete in Europe. While racing in Paris, a promoter needed spectators to easily spot the American against rivals; he created a special silk jersey with stars and stripes styled after Old Glory.

In 1933, Honeman returned home to show his talents at the new Nutley Velodrome. It had opened for races to keep up Newark's tradition. The Garden State's sports writers liked to write that cycling was New Jersey's "national" sport.

Honeman won the coveted national pro sprint championship in his stars-and-stripes jersey. Journalists and fans held him in high esteem. His jersey caught on as the official national champion's jersey, and ever since, it has designated national champions.

Nutley's track encouraged a new generation of riders. When the board oval opened, Ray Blum, a native of Nutley, began racing on the velodrome. He competed against another local, Cliff Bullivant, a great-uncle of three-time Tour de France winner Greg LeMond.

Years later, with excitement in his voice, Blum recalled hanging around outside the front of the velodrome, hoping to catch the eye of one of the visiting pros like Aussie Reggie McNamara, a tall Canadian with fiery red hair named Torchy Peden or Norman Hill of San Jose, California.

"We offered to carry their bikes; that way, we would get free entry and get to talk with these great stars," said Blum, who competed in about one thousand bike races and was a speed skater in the 1948 Winter Olympics in St. Moritz, Switzerland.

Nutley holds a unique cycling distinction. Nutley mayor Charles A. Sherwood was the 1906 national amateur sprint champion. Another distinction was that its last U.S. national pro sprint championship program in 1937 was won by world champion Mathias Engel of Cologne, Germany. When Engel retired, he operated a bike shop across the street from Nutley High School.

Nutley's track closed soon afterward, and the tradition of bicycle racing moved to Somerville where races have been held since 1940. Somerville's race director, Fred "Pop" Kugler, maneuvered to make his annual event national caliber with a generous prize list from local merchants.

The Tour of Somerville made the transition from competitors on one-speed steel track bikes to twenty-speed road machines. Winners of the fifty-mile men's criterium have set the unofficial national record (only distances on tracks are official) seventeen times. Nearly every great talent has competed around the streets of Somerville, including Tour de France winner Greg LeMond and stage winner George Hincapie.

History is a brutal editor, and much of America's cycling heritage has been shoved aside. Generations of international cyclists and their New Jersey fans have created a rich legacy. Fortunately, Michael Gabriele has applied his researching and writing talents to remind us of New Jersey's invaluable and longstanding contributions to the sport and the colorful athletes who gave it class.

Peter Joffre Nye is the author of *Hearts of Lions: The History of American Bicycle Racing*, and numerous other books on cycling.

ACKNOWLEDGEMENTS

My heartfelt thanks go to The History Press and my commissioning editor, Whitney Tarella, for giving me the opportunity to publish this book.

Special thanks to Jeff Groman and Peter Nye for their friendship, encouragement and assistance. I greatly appreciate the help of the Newark Public Library, Nutley Public Library, Nutley Historical Society, Clifton Main Memorial Library, Trenton Public Library, Princeton University Library, Rutgers University Library, Orange Public Library, Plainfield Public Library and the Atlantic City Free Public Library.

Many thanks to the organizers and directors of the Tour of Somerville (Dan Puntillo, Joe Saling, Ron Czajkowski, Vince Menci), for their support and their stewardship of an important Garden State tradition.

Thanks to John Jurich; Joseph M. Laufer; Mildred Kugler; Fawkner Crematorium and Memorial Park, Fawkner, Victoria, Australia; Jack Simes III; Phil White; Ward Miele; Laura Van Gilder; Commissioner Frank A. Cocchiola; Mayor Joanne Cocchiola; Alf Goullet; Otto Eisele; Harry Hopkins; Mary O'Neill; Frank A. Orechio; Harry Schwartzman; Walt Journey; the *Asbury Park Press*; H.B. Smith Industrial Village Conservancy; and U.S. Bicycling Hall of Fame.

This book is dedicated to my family, Julie, Michael, Charles and Ginger; and the Clifton High School Mustang Marching Band.

Introduction

"What Happened to Bike Racing?"

An article in the June 30, 1893 edition of the *New York Times*—with the headline "A Good State for Cyclists"—proclaimed New Jersey "can justly boast of having the fastest bicycle rider in the world (Arthur A. Zimmerman), the best roads in the country and the prettiest bicycle clubhouses in the Union." In short, New Jersey was identified as the cycling capital of the United States.

And so it was, as top riders, superior infrastructure, state-of-the-art velodromes and tracks and the grass-roots efforts of dedicated cycling clubs created the Garden State's grand legacy as the cradle of U.S. cycling.

There's an old saying in journalism that editors choose their stories, but sometimes stories choose their editor. The latter was true for me. I was working at the *Nutley Sun*, my hometown newspaper, in 1980, when a man walked into the office with a shoebox filled with memorabilia and asked if I would be interested in writing a story about the Nutley Velodrome. I interviewed golden-age cyclists, studied scrapbooks and library microfilm files and wrote a three-part series in the January 22 and 29 and the February 5, 1981 editions of the *Sun*.

Beginning as a national craze in the 1880s, the golden age of cycling evolved as a major spectator sport and an international enterprise, with world-class athletes competing in circuits throughout North America, Europe and Australia. Sparked by the collective efforts of wheelmen clubs and sports entrepreneurs, the Garden State—Newark in particular—was a

NEWARK VELODROME CYCLE RACING ASSOCIATION INC.

UNDER N.C.A. PERMIT

RACES BEGIN AT 8 PM

OFFICIAL 10¢ PROGRAMME

SATURDAY NIGHT, SEPTEMBER 5, 1925

OFFICIALS

REFEREE—FRANK L. KRAMER

Judges—William Drake, E. Egbert E. Christopherson, Joseph Cooney, George E. Post, Alfred Freiensehner, Roy W. Christopherson, John Friend, Jr.

Scorers and Timers—Harry V. Cole, Andrew Graef, Charles Caufield, James White.

Starter—Gabriel J. Abieneste. *Clerk of Course*—Eddie Bedford.

Announcer—William Sullivan.   *Track Surgeon*—Harvey T. Herold.

Office: 128 Market Street   Telephone, **Market 4272**   Track Telephone, **Market 9710**

Music by Joe Basile and His Popular Band.

NEXT WEDNESDAY NIGHT

AT THIS TRACK

50 MILE NATIONAL MOTOR-PACED CHAMPIONSHIP RACE, PRO.

NOTE—This is the 22nd of the Series of 24 Races to Decide the Motor-Paced Championship of America

THE STARTERS WILL BE

VINCENT MADONNA	GEORGE CHAPMAN	CHARLES VERKYN
HENRY WYNSDAU	FRANK KEENAN	CLARENCE CARMAN

Newark Velodrome program, September 5, 1925. *Courtesy of the Newark Public Library.*

hub for bicycle racing. April 16, 2011, will mark the 100th anniversary of the opening day of the Newark Velodrome.

But for all its glory, New Jersey's golden age of cycling quietly faded from memory, and few remnants were left behind. It is a forgotten history. Many of the sport's veterans I interviewed during the early 1980s remained bitter over the demise. Specific complaints were that the power brokers of the golden age lacked the vision to invest in the game and innovate and failed to develop a new generation of talent.

When pondering the disappearance of cycling's golden era, one must consider the firsthand accounts of informed observers. A headline in the April 10, 1955 edition of the *Newark Sunday News* asked the question: "What Happened to Bike Racing?" Distinguished sports journalist Willie Ratner, who penned a vast number of column inches on cycling during the golden era, was the author of the story.

There hasn't been any outdoor professional bicycle racing in New Jersey since 1937 [actually 1940] and very little anywhere in this country after that, but this veteran cycling writer and enthusiast finds the long, sustained interest in the sport even today amazing. Every year, just about this time of the season, which was when the ancient South Orange Avenue [Newark] Velodrome and later the Nutley Velodrome used to throw open the doors, old-time bike fans begin asking one another the same old question: "Do you think the bike game will ever come back?" Well, the last requiem over the bike game was sung several times, but never has there been such a lapse between revivals.

The game always proved a very lively corpse and there always was an "angel" on hand to supply fresh money and fresh lumber for a new track when old ones died out. The situation now, however, is quite different. Not only has the game died away, but the professional bike riders are gone. The veterans disappeared from the picture in a natural way, just as they would have evaporated had there been constant racing, but with no tracks on which to compete, no new riders were developed.

Were a track suddenly to spring up, the only riders available would be amateurs. From them would have to come the pros, and since the amateur field is so limited, it would take years for the professional game to become a reality again. It just doesn't seem possible for such a thing to happen.

It no longer would be possible to build wooden stands; building codes make it compulsory for promoters today to build arenas of concrete and steel. This would make the cost of an up-to-date racetrack prohibitive. It would be too great a gamble.

The golden era of American big band swing music faded in the late 1940s, but the art of jazz evolved and created new forms of expression. The golden age of professional bicycle racing ended in 1940, but the sport of cycling evolved, found new paths and flourished. In both cases, a confluence of social and economic factors spurred change. Rediscovering the Garden State's cycling heritage honors the heroes of the past, provides a deeper appreciation for current fans and participants and preserves a trust to enlighten future generations. It's safe to say New Jersey always will be at the heart of cycling's living history.

Michael C. Gabriele
December 2010

Note to readers: All towns and cities mentioned in the text are located in New Jersey unless otherwise indicated.

Chapter 1

The Dawn of an Era

An Exciting Day in Orange

There was a strange occurrence in Orange on Thursday, January 30, 1879. A man on a high-wheel bicycle was riding along the boulevards, waving to curious passersby. It was a sight few had ever seen, and according to a report in the town newspaper, it created "quite an excitement" on the usually quiet streets.

"The main wheel, nearly five feet in diameter, upon which the rider's saddle rests, is composed of double spokes made from the finest steel," the *Orange Journal* reported in its February 1, 1879 edition. "The tire is soft rubber. There is a small balance wheel in the rear. The perfect ease with which this machine is propelled over our macadam roads indicates the useful purposes to which it may be applied.

"Our young friend, Llewellyn H. Johnson of West Orange, is the owner of the bicycle," the article stated. Johnson would go on to become a sales agent for Columbia bicycles as well as prove himself to be an accomplished rider, winning a two-mile race during the Staten Island Athletic Club's spring games, held May 24, 1879, at the one-sixth-mile oval (with a surface of hard-rolled cinder) in West Brighton, Staten Island.

Ten years earlier, in Orange, there were "highly entertaining exhibitions" of wooden-wheel "bone-shaker" bicycles. The *Orange Chronicle*, in its February 13, 1869 edition, said people flocked to Liberty Hall "last night and the previous evening" to witness a "new-fashioned locomotive arrangement known as the velocipede."

On May 31 and July 12, 1879, the Short Hills Athletic Club of New Jersey hosted two-mile bicycle races on the town's athletic grounds, located along the Delaware, Lackawanna and Western Railroad line. A network of bicycling enthusiasm was taking root throughout the Garden State.

This was the dawn of New Jersey's golden age of cycling.

WAVERLY

The Waverly Fairgrounds of Newark became a site for bicycle racing in the late 1870s. In addition to hosting state agricultural fairs, Waverly featured a half-mile, horse-trotting oval, which was used by the bike racers. Weequahic Park, the 311-acre site designed by the Olmstead Brothers, in the city's South Ward, which sits between Route 22 and Newark Airport, today occupies what was the Waverly Fairgrounds.

The Essex Bicycle Club organized a three-mile race at Waverly on June 12, 1879, the *Times* reported. On September 18, 1879, twenty thousand people attended the state fair, with events that included a bicycle race. The twenty-seventh annual fair of the New Jersey Agricultural Society, on September

Weequahic Park, dated June 13, 1932. *Courtesy of Jeff Groman, Jazz Sport LLC.*

18, 1885, had several cycling competitions: a three-mile race; a state club championship, one-mile race; and two other one-mile races. The Riverside Athletic Club of Newark sponsored its first meet on October 16, 1892. The Riverside club—led by President John K. Gore, Vice-President C.D. Karr and Treasurer John D. Mills—also sanctioned cycling meets on July 16 and August 26, 1893.

The League of American Wheelmen sponsored a two-mile race on August 30, 1893, offering seventy-five dollars in prizes. The Metropolitan Association of Cycling Clubs—an umbrella group representing twenty-five bicycling organizations—selected Waverly for a major meet on September 16, 1893.

"Waverly is a station on the Pennsylvania Railroad, five minutes from Newark and 35 minutes from New York City," the *Times* explained in a September 9, 1893 story. "A special race train will be run on race day, leaving (New York) at 1:50 and arriving on time for the first race (on Sept. 16)."

On June 16, 1894, the Elizabeth Athletic Cyclers sponsored an eight-race meet at Waverly that drew riders from the New York Athletic Club, the Tourist Cycle Club, the Crescent Wheelmen, the Riverside Wheelmen, the Bedford Cycle Club, the Washington Wheelmen and the Montclair Wheelmen. Waverly also hosted top professional cyclists. A meet on August 14, 1897, featured Eddie Bald of Buffalo, New York, and Tom Cooper of Detroit—two U.S. champions. With four thousand spectators cheering him on, Bald won the featured event—a one-mile open pro race. In the five-mile professional race, Nat Butler of Cambridge, Massachusetts, prevailed in a field of thirty-five riders.

PARADES

Bicycle riders from Orange, Newark, Hoboken, New Brunswick, Plainfield and Smithville, bedecked in their colorful club uniforms, crossed the Hudson River on Monday, May 28, 1883, to take part in a bicycle parade along Fifth Avenue in New York City. The League of American Wheelmen, founded on May 30, 1880, in Newport, Rhode Island, organized the gala event. The procession stepped off at 3:00 p.m. with 750 cyclists riding in formation. Most riders mounted high-wheel "Ordinary" bikes, while others chose "comfortable and exceedingly stable" tricycles, the *New York Times* reported. Seven years later, the League of American Wheelmen had grown to over 100,000 members.

Jersey City staged a bicycle parade on August 29, 1896, a gathering of 1,500 riders that included 200 women cyclists. The parade traveled along Hudson Boulevard to West Newark Avenue. Mayors Peter F. Wanser (of Jersey City), Mark M. Fagan (of Hoboken) and Egbert Seymour (of Bayonne) reviewed the parade. Earlier that same year, on March 3, members of the Hudson County Wheelmen celebrated their fourteenth anniversary at the group's Jersey City clubhouse, located at 111 Belmont Avenue.

ROSEVILLE

The New Jersey Cycling and Athletic Association opened a cycling track in the Roseville section of Newark on Saturday, September 4, 1886. The first-day program, which drew two thousand fans, included eleven races. J.B. Pearson of the Vineland Bicycle Club won the featured match, the three-mile championship of New Jersey, and took home a solid-silver cup. E.P. Baird of the Orange Wanderers placed second.

The Roseville track, with a rolled surface comprised of potter's clay and gravel, was located on Park Avenue. Fencing was built on the inner and outer perimeters of the track to separate riders and spectators. There was grandstand seating for 1,000 fans, plus bleachers that could hold another 1,500 patrons.

The inaugural race set the stage for a three-day cycling tournament, sponsored by the athletic association, held from September 30 to October 2, 1886. Two hundred bike riders signed up to compete in the tournament, which offered $2,000 in prizes. The lead story on the front page of the September 28, 1886 edition of the *Newark Evening News* stated that a temporary train station was built at North Thirteenth Street and Park Avenue on the now-defunct Bloomfield/Montclair branch of the Delaware, Lackawanna and Western (DL&W) railroad line, just four blocks from the track, to accommodate patrons.

Four thousand fans, including "gaily attired ladies," turned out for the opening of the tournament, which featured the music of Markwith's Orange Fifth Regiment band to serenade the festivities. "Long before the hour set for the initial performance, Park Avenue presented a charming picture, with its crowds of cyclists whirling silently toward the scene of the contest," the *News* reported on page one of its October 1, 1886 edition. "Additional trains were run on the (DL&W) railroad, bearing loads of lovers of the now-famous pastime."

The Dawn of an Era

George M. Hendee of Springfield, Massachusetts, America's first national amateur champion, won gold medals in two "promateur" events—a one-mile race on September 30 and three-mile race on October 1. The *News* reported that Charles H. Frazier of Smithfield captured the "most exciting struggle" of opening day—a ten-mile pro match. Frazier defeated British cycling champion Fred Wood of Leicester, England, "by a wheel." Races at Roseville continued through 1887.

IRVINGTON-MILLBURN

A series of ten-mile road races, between the towns of Millburn and Irvington, was organized in the mid-1880s. According to the archives of the Millburn Free Public Library, local newspapers reported that one race was held on August 18, 1886. A twenty-five-mile version of the contest, which became known as the Irvington-Millburn race and dubbed a "national" event, took place on Memorial Day (known in that era as "Decoration Day," which originally referred to the decoration of graves of Civil War soldiers), May 30, 1889.

The May 30, 1900 Irvington-Millburn race attracted 119 competitors of "almost every age, size, nationality and color," from as far east as Boston and as far south as Philadelphia, the *Times* reported. Fifteen thousand fans lined the five miles of country roads between the two villages. Edgar Van Velsor, a "red-headed, sturdy-limbed" rider from Oyster Bay, Long Island, was the winner. His prize was a $250 piano. David Turner of Paterson was the winner of the May 30, 1901 race.

THE ATALANTA WHEELMEN

In the 1880s and 1890s, influential cycling organizations, led by the League of American Wheelmen (today known as the League of American Bicyclists), promoted the sport in their respective communities and lobbied elected officials for better roadways and safety laws—the "Good Roads Movement."

The New Jersey Historic Bridge Survey, a report prepared by A.G. Lichtenstein & Associates Inc. in September 1994 for the state's Department of Transportation, declared

Organizations like the Essex Bicycle Club, the Atalanta Wheelmen and the Trenton Wheelmen created the social network that promoted the sport of cycling in the 1880s and sparked the Good Roads Movement. *Courtesy of the Newark Public Library.*

it was the two-wheeled conveyance that sparked the Good Roads Movement. The League of American Wheelmen claimed that good highways would raise property values, open new markets, provide access to manufactured goods, end rural poverty, increase political participation by farmers and improve education.

The report said New Jersey, in 1891, became the first in the nation to establish a state-aided, road-building program, "a milestone in the history of highway administration in the United States."

The Essex Bicycle Club, founded March 8, 1879, was the first group organized in the Garden State and one of the first in the country. *The American Bicycler*, a book by Charles E. Pratt, said the group's headquarters was located at 766 Broad Street, Newark. (Pratt was a founding father of the League of American Wheelmen.)

The Essex club selected Joseph Lafon as its first president, Herbert W. Knight as its secretary and treasurer and Llewellyn H. Johnson—the iconic rider of Orange—as captain. The *Orange Journal*, in its May 24, 1879, edition,

The Bay View Wheelmen club was organized on July 29, 1897. The clubhouse was located at 380 South Sixth Street in Newark. *Courtesy of Jeff Groman, Jazz Sport LLC.*

reported that the group held an evening meeting in Newark on May 12 and selected the club's uniform: a dark blue flannel jacket and polo cap, with light-gray corduroy knickerbockers and stockings. One year later, the Orange Wanderers were formed as a branch of the Essex Bicycle Club, to be followed by the Orange Wheelmen in 1890. The Orange Athletic Club Cyclers, formed in 1893, operated the quarter-mile Orange Oval track in East Orange. Newark's Bay View Wheelmen club was founded on July 29, 1897.

The Atalanta Wheelmen—named for the Greek goddess of the hunt, travel and adventure—was formed in Newark on March 11, 1886, at the home of Arthur W. Snow. William V. Belknap was interviewed by the *Times* for its May 26, 1894 edition to recall the genesis of the Atalanta organization. Newark, he said, never was slow to embrace things that were "bicyclistic" during the 1880s. As the number of "pedal pushers" rapidly grew, he said it was natural for these like-minded sportsmen to band together for "mutual aid, protection and consolation. In union there is strength."

Newark, at the time, benefited from an extensive network of well-paved macadam roadways—an attractive infrastructure to encourage cycling.

"Good roads and wheeling go hand in hand," Belknap pointed out. "As the years rolled by the wheel (bicycle) improved very perceptively in workmanship and with the improvement came popularity and with popularity appeared numerous clubs."

In early 1886, a collection of seven "ardent wheelmen" in Newark, who had remained aloof from existing clubs, decided to form their own alliance. "After much palaver, a club was formed (on March 11) and the debate over an appropriate name for the organization was long and heated," Belknap said. "Finally, a member was consulted who was well versed in mythological lore and his proposal of assuming the name of that fleet-footed goddess Atalanta, who could outrun all the young men of the time, met with enthusiastic and hilarious approval."

Having agreed upon a name for the club, a constitution and bylaws were drafted, and officers were elected: William S. Gregory, president; Charles A. Woodruff, vice-president; Wilbur F. Coddington, secretary and treasurer; Arthur W. Snow, captain; and Samuel Drabble, lieutenant.

Within two years the group grew to 28 members while organizing an increasing number of club rides and sanctioning races. In need of a permanent headquarters to house club activities, the Atalanta Wheelmen purchased a three-story brownstone, 50 Clinton Street, in November 1891. The club's headcount at this point was in excess of 130. (The Clinton Street building is no longer there; the site is now occupied by a parking lot.)

THE TRI-STATE RELAY RACE

On July 15, 1893, the Atalanta Wheelmen organized a one-hundred-mile, round-trip, Newark-to-Princeton race through the pastoral New Jersey Sourlands, an event that attracted 112 riders. Jacob W. Linneman of the Press Cycling Club of Buffalo, New York, won the "century run," while J.T. Marshall of the Atalanta club finished second.

Looking to create an even grander spectacle for cycling in the Garden State, the Atalanta Wheelmen organized a tri-state relay race—a collection of three six-man teams, representing New Jersey, New York and Pennsylvania. The race, which was held on June 2, 1894, stretched 150 miles in six 25-mile stages, from New York to Philadelphia. The *Times* was an enthusiastic supporter of the event, providing extensive coverage, medals and trophies.

"The start will be made from the *New York Times* office at 8 a.m. and it is expected that the race will be finished in Philadelphia between 5 and 6 o'clock in the evening," the *Times* reported. For members of the winning team, the *Times* provided "two-bar" medals that featured silver bars, gold chains and a solid-gold eagle.

Teams were a collection of all-star cyclists from each state. E.L. Blauvelt of the Elizabeth Athletic Club and the Newark Wheelmen, W.C. Roome of the Hudson County Wheelmen and F.J. MacMahon of the Tourist Cycling Club of Paterson were the top riders on the New Jersey squad. Teams wore sashes to identify their riders: red for New Jersey, blue for New York and white for Pennsylvania. Thousands of fans lined the roadways of the Garden State, as riders rolled through the towns of Paterson, Boonton, Morristown, Springfield, Plainfield, Elizabeth, Rahway, New Brunswick and Trenton. Cheered on by the home-state crowds, the New Jersey team won the race. The winners received their medals from the *Times* during a boisterous reception at the Atalanta clubhouse on the evening of June 8, 1894.

The 150-mile event was reprised on June 8, 1895, billed as the *New York Times* Tri-State Relay Race. This time, the Hudson County Wheelmen managed the event. Once again, the Garden State team prevailed. In a ceremony held June 20, the victorious riders received medals and trophies, again provided by the *Times*, at the Hudson County Wheelmen's headquarters in Jersey City. Members of the winning team included Thomas Hughes of the East Side Wheelmen of Paterson; William Slain of the Tourist Cycle Club of Paterson; A.J. Hargan and William Welles, both of the Century Cycle Club of Newark; F.G. Smith of the Bloomfield Cycling and Athletic Association; and Simpson Standeven, Active Athletic Club of Paterson.

Atalanta members were influential in business and racing circles. Carl Von Lengerke was secretary of the Associated Cycling Clubs of New Jersey and the Newark representative of the Metropolitan Association of Cycling Clubs. Frank L.C. Martin of Plainfield was "the pioneer bicycle dealer of New Jersey," according to *The History of Union County, New Jersey.*

Born in Brooklyn, New York, in 1865, Martin grew up in the Plainfield area and began his business career in 1881, working for a Wall Street brokerage firm and later an insurance company. During the late 1880s, Martin pursued his interest in the bicycle business, and by 1893, he had become involved in ventures in New Brunswick, East Orange, Westfield, Newark and Plainfield. The Plainfield operation eventually was incorporated under the name F.L.C. Martin Cycle Co. A six-column display ad in the June 4, 1897 edition of the *Union County Standard* touted Martin's business as "the oldest bicycle house in New Jersey."

By the late winter of 1895, the Atalanta club determined it was time to reorganize "in order to get rid of passive and derelict members and bolster the treasury," the *Times* reported on March 6, 1895. "At present, there are 85 members…and each one will be assessed $5."

On March 11, 1926, the Atalanta group celebrated its fortieth anniversary at the Newark Athletic Club, a reunion that made page one of the *Newark Evening News*. The gathering drew thirty-four old-timers—dressed in tuxedoes—including William A. Drabble, who served as president of the group and presided at the dinner. "The Atalanta Wheelmen were the elite in bicycle road riding circles (in Newark) in the latter part of the last century, when riding was at its height," the story stated. "To sport the colors (gold and blue) of the Atalanta Wheelmen was to sit on top of the world of cycling in Newark."

TRENTON, ASBURY PARK AND PLAINFIELD

Trenton, Plainfield and Asbury Park spawned bicycle clubs and hosted major races. According to information posted on the Trenton Historical Society's website, cycling enthusiasts founded the Trenton Bicycle Club on June 12, 1884. S.S. Staples was tapped as the first president of the club. In September 1885, the group moved into a clubhouse located at 107 East Hanover Street, on the second floor of the Old Arcade Building. A year later, the club relocated to 25 East State Street and was reorganized as the Trenton Wheelmen on November 3, 1887, electing C.T. Sutphin as its leader.

Former members of the Trenton Bicycle Club organized the Mercer County Wheelmen on November 13, 1889, with Charles Perrine as the first president. By November 1894, the Mercer group had grown to three hundred members and moved to 219 East State Street.

On Saturday, July 1, 1893, the half-mile track at Trenton's Inter-State Fairgrounds hosted the tenth Columbian meet of the New Jersey Division of the League of American Wheelmen. Arthur A. Zimmerman, racing under the colors of the Asbury Park Wheelmen and just back from a European racing tour, won the three New Jersey division championship gold medals (half-mile, mile and five-mile), while the Union County Roadsters garnered a silver loving cup (donated by the *Times*) as the cycling club with the biggest cumulative point total. Dr. G. Carleton Brown, head of the New Jersey division, presided at the award ceremonies.

Right: Mercer County Wheelmen clubhouse, 1890. *Courtesy of the Trenton Public Library.*

Below: Mercer County Wheelmen, 1894. *Courtesy of the Trenton Public Library.*

Mercer County Wheelmen, 1894. *Courtesy of the Trenton Public Library.*

The Mercer County club hosted a cycling meet at the fairgrounds on August 25, 1894, which drew more than two hundred riders. The Riverside Wheelmen of New York prevailed in the featured event on the schedule: a one-mile team race sponsored by the *New York Times*.

The Asbury Park Wheelmen, organized on September 24, 1890, sponsored its first cycling event on Thanksgiving Day that year and sanctioned races throughout the decade. Alfred C. Atkins was the first president, while William H. Stauffer served as vice president. On June 21, 1893, the wheelmen dedicated a two-mile bicycle runway that went along the beach between Asbury Park and Avon-by-the-Sea. James Adam Bradley, the New York businessman who founded Asbury Park in 1871, built the runway. The *Times* reported that over two hundred cyclists participated in a parade to celebrate the runway's opening.

By the summer of 1893, the Asbury Park Wheelmen had grown to one hundred members, compared with twenty at the first meeting. The group had the good fortune of frequently showcasing Zimmerman. Eddie Bald also made several appearances. Zimmerman, who resided in Freehold and represented the Asbury Park Wheelmen, competed at Asbury Park on August

The Dawn of an Era

Two organizations in Red Bank were active in cycling activities: the Monmouth Wheelmen, formed on August 29, 1883, and the Red Bank Athletic Club. Bike riders (the organization wasn't identified) are pictured in front of the Red Bank Police Station, 1886. *Courtesy of the Asbury Park Press.*

6, 1892, before a crowd of five thousand fans. He won the quarter-mile, one-mile and five-mile events. His winnings that day included a gold watch and gold-cuff buttons; a hammerless shotgun and revolver; and a $700 piano, an organ and a banjo. Zimmerman also was victorious in Asbury Park races held July 22 and 29, 1893. During those two meets, he won the quarter-mile, one-mile and five-mile races and, once again, garnered a king's ransom of prizes: diamond rings and pins; gold and silver watches; a gold chain; an onyx clock; and a silver tea set.

The banked track at the grounds of the Asbury Park Athletic Association was the site of races. "This populous summer city has taken on a new lease on life through the advent of racing...and the extensive crowds that follow," the *Times* wrote on September 1, 1894, saying that "hundreds" of fans were drawn to Asbury Park from the surrounding seaside resort towns to witness bicycle racing. Concert bands often performed during cycling meets. "This cycling set is a jolly one." The routes leading to the racing grounds were "lined with festive peanut vendors, milk-shake men and organette grinders with capacious hats. They all did a thriving business."

The Crescent Wheelmen of Plainfield invested $5,000 to build the Crescent Oval, a one-third-of-a-mile, banked clay and gravel track, which opened on Saturday, June 2, 1894. The *Plainfield Daily Press*, in its June 4, 1894, edition,

Street scene in Red Bank, circa 1897. Note the lone bike rider in the lower right corner. *Courtesy of the* Asbury Park Press.

reported 1,300 fans—many from outside the Union County community—turned out for opening day. Cycling aficionados from New York City and northern New Jersey could easily reach Plainfield via the Central Railroad of New Jersey. The *Daily Press* article stated the many visiting "cycling experts commented very favorably on the shape and construction of the track."

The oval's first meet attracted 126 riders from New York; Brooklyn; Springfield, Massachusetts; Providence, Rhode Island; as well as members of wheelmen clubs throughout New Jersey. The teardrop-shaped track, designed and built by F.A. Dunham, was located at the intersection of Hillside Avenue and Randolph Road. B. Jacobus of the Montclair Wheelmen won the first event, a one-mile novice match.

W.H. Rogers (president), L.B. Woolston (vice-president), J.A. Haynes (captain) and C.E. Teel (secretary) were the leaders of the Crescent Wheelmen. "No club in the state has a more representative list of members and none perhaps that is quite so influential in the social, political and business circles," the *Times* wrote in its September 28, 1894 edition. In addition to funding the construction of the oval, the Crescent Wheelmen promoted cycling as a summer-resort attraction for Plainfield. Visitors from Philadelphia and New York would travel to Plainfield by rail to ride bicycles along the well-trimmed bridle paths of the community.

The Crescent Oval opened its second season on May 30, 1895, before a crowd of three thousand. L.G. Hoppe of Brooklyn's Liberty Wheelmen won the featured final event of the day, a one-mile race. Hoppe's prize was a fifty-dollar gold medal donated by the *Times*. On September 26, 1896, Tom Cooper and Eddie Bald were the featured contestants at the oval, with Cooper winning the one-mile race and Bald taking the half-mile sprint.

PRINCETON AND RUTGERS

Students at Princeton University formed a bicycle club in 1879, which was designed to "do all that can be done to render bicycling a recognized and popular sport in Princeton," according to an October 10, 1879 installment

The Princeton University bicycle team, circa 1902. *Courtesy of Princeton University Archives at Princeton University Library.*

in the *Daily Princetonian*, the university's student newspaper. Two weeks later, the publication reported the new cycling club was flourishing. On November 5, 1879, the club organized a one-mile race, which was won by a student named Strong, a member of the class of 1881.

Rutgers College (now university), New Brunswick, also demonstrated its student cycling spirit. The February 29, 1884 edition of the *Rutgers Targum* reported that campus wheelmen met at 123 George Street. The *Targum*'s October 10, 1884 edition spelled out the constitution of the new Rutgers College Bicycle Club. Monthly dues were twenty-five cents. The regulation club uniform was a light-gray Bedford blouse, gray knee breeches and stockings, a gray tie and bicycle cap and a white flannel shirt. By 1893, cycling events were included in the Rutgers' track team's Field Day competitions.

The Princeton Tigers won the second intercollegiate cycling championship on May 30, 1900, at Woodside Park, Philadelphia, beating teams from Yale, Columbia, Pennsylvania and Swarthmore. Bert Ripley, the team captain, was the most valuable rider, winning the one-mile and half-mile matches and placing second in the five-mile race. According to the online version of

Rutgers College track and field team, pictured in the school's 1895 *Scarlet Letter* yearbook. Bicycle races were included in the team's Field Day competitions. *Courtesy of Rutgers University Libraries, Special Collections and University Archives.*

the book, *Athletics at Princeton: A History*, by Frank Presbrey and James Hugh Moffatt, Princeton finished second (to Yale) in the first intercollegiate race in 1899, also at Woodside Park; the team placed second again to Yale in 1901, in a match held at the Berkeley Oval in New York City. Ripley, a member of Princeton's class of 1901, was the star rider for the Orange and Black in all three intercollegiate competitions.

In addition to his exploits as the leader of Princeton's cycling team, Ripley was a prolific amateur rider who competed throughout the Garden State in the late 1890s. On August 10, 1895, three thousand fans at the Clifton Race Track cheered as Ripley won the one-mile open and one-mile Class A matches and placed second in the quarter-mile open. The Tourist Cycle Club of Paterson sponsored the meet. A week later in Asbury Park, he captured the one-mile, Class A lap race. He traveled to Plainfield's Crescent Oval on September 2 and, sponsored by the Harlem Wheelmen, won a one-mile race while placing second in the two-thirds-of-a-mile and two-mile matches.

Returning to the Clifton track on May 30, 1896, Ripley, sponsored by Newark's Vim Bicycle Club, placed first in the quarter-mile and one-mile matches. The Excelsior Boat Club of Paterson sponsored the event. Five thousand fans at Paterson's Tourist Oval, on August 8, watched as Ripley garnered the one-third mile state championship. However, he shared the spotlight that day with Boonton's Ray Dawson, who was sponsored by the Tourist club. Dawson captured first place in one-mile, two-mile and five-mile League of American Wheelmen state division championships.

Ripley's greatest day as an amateur was September 18, 1897, racing at Waverly Park. In a meet sponsored by the League of American Wheelmen, he won state championship titles in the quarter-mile, the half-mile and one-mile matches. Dawson won the state two-mile championship that day.

Bertram Reynold Ripley was born on February 18, 1875, and attended schools in Newark. After graduating from Princeton, he joined his family's business, David Ripley & Sons Lumber Co., an enterprise founded by his grandfather, which was based in Newark. He put away his bicycle and focused on his business career for the next eighteen years. Tragically, he took his own life on January 25, 1919, according to biographical information provided by Princeton University's Rare Books and Special Collections and Seeley G. Mudd Manuscript Library.

The American Star

The H.B. Smith Machine Co. of Smithville, a manufacturer of woodworking machinery, briefly dabbled in the production of the American Star high-wheel bicycle in the 1880s. The ratchet-drive Star, originally patented by George W. Pressey of Hammonton, reversed the configuration of the typical Ordinary high-wheel bicycle by using the small wheel as the front wheel of the bicycle to provide safer steering.

Joseph M. Laufer, president of the H.B. Smith Industrial Village Conservancy and the Burlington County historian, said J.J. White—a cranberry bog farmer of New Lisbon whose company was the first to cultivate the wild blueberry—introduced Pressey to industrialist Hezekiah Bradley Smith in December 1880, shortly after Pressey received his patent for the bicycle. White was a member of Smith Machine's board of directors and knew Smith was looking to diversify his operations.

The first Star prototype was built on January 26, 1881. The Star's development phase continued slowly for the next two years, as there were

A worker at the H.B. Smith Machine Co. of Smithville displays the American Star bicycle. *Courtesy of Joseph M. Laufer, H.B. Smith Industrial Village Conservancy.*

flaws in the bicycle's initial design as well as problems retrofitting Smith's production equipment. William Kelley, a top engineer at H.B. Smith Machine Co., took charge of the project and patented his own design improvements, which eventually created legal squabbles between Pressey and Smith Machine. A major challenge in the manufacturing process was the production of the bicycle's steel spokes.

Citing conservancy archives, Laufer said 38 Star cycles were produced between September 1882 and September 1883; 237 were built in the next twelve-month period. The *Mount Holly Herald*, in its December 15, 1883 edition, reported the Smith Machine Co.'s bicycle division was "very busy" and had received an order for 100 Star cycles. The newspaper, in February 1885, reported bookings for 106 and 300 Star cycles.

Smith Machine began to phase out production of the bicycle in 1886, though it continued to market the Star for the next three years. Laufer estimated that, overall, two thousand American Star cycles were built. There were at least six distinct models in the series, and they sold in a range of $75 to $150 per unit. Though production was short-lived, Laufer said Smith Machine developed innovative ways to market the Star, which was touted as a precision racing bike. Acrobats were hired to ride the Star down the steps of the Capitol in Washington, D.C., to demonstrate its balance and safety, while famous racers, such as George E. Weber—the 1885 half-mile American cycling champion—lent their sporting celebrity status to endorse the Star.

Advertising poster of the American Star bicycle. *Courtesy of Joseph M. Laufer, H.B. Smith Industrial Village Conservancy.*

An Electric Symbol

British bicycles were prominently displayed at the Centennial International Exhibition, which opened in Philadelphia on May 10, 1876. In later years, professional trade shows helped to define the sport and business of bicycle racing. The Associated Cycling Club (ACC) of Philadelphia, a group organized in March 1888 and comprised of eleven of the city's largest bicycle clubs, staged the ACC Cycle Show in March 1891 in Horticultural Hall.

The Philadelphia show proved to be so popular that the ACC moved the venue to Philadelphia's larger Industrial Hall the following year (February 15–22, 1892). The purpose of the event, according to notes in the 1892 souvenir program, was to host

> *a thoroughly representative exhibition of the cycling trade of the country; to show the advances made in the manufacture of bicycles and their accessories. The making of bicycles is now a legitimate manufacturing interest in which thousands of skilled laborers are employed and millions of capital invested.*

The ACC program went on to praise cycling's "liberation" of female riders. "The woman who has never been on wheels has missed half her life. At first there was a great amount of prejudice against cycling for women. Time has, as usual, proved the best advocate of the cause."

New York put together its own grand exhibition at Madison Square Garden in 1894 and followed up with a second show at the same site in January 1895. The *Times*, in a January 13, 1895 story, stated the weeklong exhibit at the Garden featured 150 exhibitors and drew eighty thousand visitors.

The 1895 Madison Square Garden event showcased a dazzling presentation—an electric sign in the amphitheater that measured 108 feet in length, 35 feet in width, with 2,192 lamps. The focal point of the sign was the illuminated image of a bicycle, a graphic representation 20 feet long and 13 feet high. "Colored lights will be artistically arranged for the different parts (of the bicycle)." The electric sign provided eye-popping glitz for the exhibition and conveyed a more profound, underlying message: cycling was now part of the American consciousness as an important sport, leisure/social activity and business.

The Garden's third bicycle show opened on January 18, 1896, under the auspices of the National Board of Trade and, again, was ablaze with imaginative displays of electric lights. A guest of honor was Colonel Albert Pope, who founded the Pope Manufacturing Co. in 1877 and, one year later, introduced the Columbia line of bicycles. "Nineteen years ago I began the manufacture of cycles and, sanguine as I then was, I never dared to dream that the business would develop into anything like it now is," Pope told the *Times*. "Young men used to save up their money to buy a horse or a watch; now they save to buy a bicycle."

The trade shows in New York and Philadelphia reflected the growing awareness of the business opportunities tied to the sport. The *Times*, in an article published June 28, 1896, estimated there were four million American cyclists who had invested $300 million in their bicycles, $10 million in cycling clothing and $200 million in sundries and repairs. There were, at the time, 250 bicycle manufacturers (employing seventy-five thousand workers) and 5 major tire producers (three thousand employees).

Newark, affectionately known as "Brick City," was a vibrant center for manufacturing bicycle components in the 1880s and 1890s. "In many factories of this city, parts of bicycles are made to supply some of the well-known manufacturers," the *Newark Evening News* reported in its June 2, 1897 edition. "One firm in this city makes all of the pedals used on one of wheels best known both on the track and road, and other factories produce cones, tubes and wheels."

BIKES ON THE BOARDWALK

The Atlantic City Coliseum Cycling Track opened on May 29, 1902. Investors from New York and Baltimore built the structure, which was located on the boardwalk between Massachusetts and Connecticut Avenues, a site previously occupied by the seaside resort's popular Japanese Tea Gardens. Arthur A. Irwin, a New York sportsman and former major league baseball player, served as manager of the coliseum.

The outdoor track—seven laps to a mile with sharp, banked curves—was designed to feature motor-pace racing. Motor-pace was a popular event that paired a motorcycle driver with a trailing bicycle racer, pedaling in the "draft," or slipstream. The *Atlantic City Daily Press* and the *Evening Union* reported a crowd of 2,500 watched as Benny Munroe of Memphis, Tennessee, won the featured twenty-mile motor-pace race on opening night.

There was a tragic accident leading up to the debut of the track. Archie McEachern, a champion bike rider from Toronto, was killed on May 13, 1902, during a motor-pace practice run, according to a biography of the cyclist written by Arnold Devlin on the 6-Day Racing website. McEachern, age twenty-eight, was thrown from his bike and suffered massive injuries. He died at Atlantic City Hospital, the *Daily Press* reported.

Races at the coliseum were discontinued during World War I. The *Times* reported that William "Torchy" Peden and Franco Georgetti, professional cyclists from Canada and Italy, respectively, teamed up to win a six-day race at Atlantic City's Convention Hall that ended on July 9, 1932.

Chapter 2

NEWARK:
THE CENTER STAGE

VAILSBURG

A group of investors, looking to seize upon the potential of cycling as a business venture and spectator sport, in the spring of 1897 unveiled plans to create a velodrome in Vailsburg—at the time an independent borough, which was annexed on January 1, 1905, by Newark. Vailsburg today is a distinct neighborhood in the city's West Ward.

A corporation known as the New Jersey Bicycle Track Co., headed by Henry J. and Charles B. Bloemecke, would build the saucer. The group formed an alliance with the Vim Bicycle Club of Newark to promote races. The Vailsburg board track, as it came to be known, would be a quarter-mile oval located on the south side of South Orange Avenue.

"Ground will be broken this week for the construction of a new bicycle track that will be thoroughly up to date," the Monday, May 10, 1897 edition of the *News* reported. "A grandstand capable of seating 2,000 persons will also be built along with two big open stands." The *Times*, in a May 16 story, said the track's surface would be constructed of yellow pine, tongued and grooved, with leaded joints to reduce vibration. Both newspapers indicated the design of the Vailsburg oval would be modeled after the Memphis Velodrome, which was built by British sports promoter John Shillington Prince.

The *News* updated progress on the construction of the site throughout the month of May, reporting (on May 25) that over one hundred men worked through the night, aiming to complete the track by Memorial Day.

Postcard of Vailsburg board track, dated November 9, 1905. *Courtesy of Jeff Groman, Jazz Sport LLC.*

The Vailsburg track opened on May 31, 1897, and drew one thousand spectators, but news coverage indicated construction of the wooden oval was not yet finished. "The track was in good shape," the *News* article stated, but "no seats had been erected and the spectators had to stand up on the outer edge of the track or sit down on it. Many stood in the muddy circle (infield) inside."

Opening day was billed as a meet of the Century Cycle Club, assisted by the race committee of the Vim Bicycle Club. The first heat of the first race, a one-mile novice match, was won by a cyclist named Stan Baldwin of Bloomfield who "pedaled to the music of a band" in the saucer. J.H. Lake was victorious in the one-mile open race.

Bicycle racing at the Waverly Fairgrounds continued despite the arrival of the Vailsburg track. Races at Waverly held on Vailsburg's opening day drew over 3,500 spectators. The Atalanta Wheelmen sponsored the May 31 meet for amateur and professional cyclists.

ZIMMY

Arthur Augustus Zimmerman was the featured attraction on opening day at the Vailsburg oval. "Zimmy, who had not been on a track for a long time… was greeted with cheers," the *News* reported. He performed a half-mile exhibition, paced by the Vim team.

Born in Camden on June 11, 1869 (some sources say 1870), Zimmerman was an international sports celebrity, with successful cycling tours of Europe and Australia from 1892 to 1895. "Jerseymen point to their fellow citizen with feelings of pride," the *Times* wrote about Zimmerman in June 30, 1893, referring to him as one reason New Jersey was considered the top cycling state in the nation. "His name is a household word wherever the wheel is seen. He only came into prominence a few years ago, but in that short time he has whipped the champions of France, England and Ireland and today is regarded as the peer of any man in the world."

His banner year was 1893, when he won a series of championship events held in the Midwest. Zimmerman began the campaign in New Jersey by winning three races on

Arthur A. Zimmerman, circa 1893. *Courtesy of the collection of Lorne Shields, Toronto, Ontario, Canada.*

July 1, 1893, in Trenton, hosted by the New Jersey Division of the League of American Wheelmen. Three days later, ten thousand fans turned out at the Clifton Race Track to watch Zimmerman, the "Jersey Skeeter," win four races—the three-quarter mile, the quarter mile, the mile and two mile—in a meet sponsored by the Tourist Cycle Club of Paterson. Later that month, he won several races at Asbury Park.

Traveling west, he won a three-mile lap race in Detroit on August 1. He then arrived in Chicago to compete in the World's Fair Cycling Tournament and First International Race Meet, the fourteenth annual meet sponsored by the League of American Wheelmen, held August 5–12, 1893. Races took place during the 1893 World's Columbian Exhibition (world's fair), which opened on May 1 in Chicago.

Matches were held at Chicago's South Side Ball Park. Over a five-day period (August 8–12), dispatches from the *Times* reported Zimmy dominated the field, winning the quarter-mile national championship, the one-mile Ordinary national championship, the quarter-mile open championship, the one-mile (Safety) national championship, the half-mile open championship, the ten-kilometer national championship and the one-mile international championship—the victory that earned him the crown of world champion. He also took second place in the five-mile national championship.

Moving on to Milwaukee's half-mile track at National Park for an "international meet," Zimmerman raced under the colors of the New York Athletic Club and won half-mile and one-mile events on August 14, 1893. He capped off his extraordinary Midwest swing by winning the one-mile World's Championship Cup on August 24, 1893, at the Indianapolis State Fair Grounds, a meet sponsored by that city's Zigzag Cycling Club.

In April 1894, Zimmerman announced he would leave the amateur ranks and become a professional. The *Times*, on April 13, 1894, reported that he had accepted a $10,000 offer, plus other considerations, from the Union Velocipedeque Francais to race in France. On April 16, 1894, two days before he set sail for Europe, the League of American Wheelmen hosted a dinner to honor Zimmerman at New York's Hotel Bartholdi, which was located at Broadway and Twenty-third Street. Howard E. Raymond, chairman of the league's racing board, presided at the event. Benjamin Pitman, who won the first-ever organized U.S. bicycle race at a Boston meet in 1878, was the keynote speaker. Nye wrote that Zimmerman had a successful tour, dazzling the crowds at Paris's Buffalo Velodrome.

During his career, Zimmerman made the transition to a Safety (a modern bicycle) from the high-wheel Ordinary. On June 27, 1891, he won the one-mile Ordinary championship of America, racing before a crowd of two thousand spectators at the tenth annual games of the Kings County Wheelmen, held at Washington Park, Brooklyn, New York. Zimmerman was the star of the annual meet, sponsored by the Elizabeth Wheelmen and held September 26, 1891, at the New Jersey Jockey Club's grounds. Riding a Safety bicycle, he won the one-mile and two-mile handicap matches, starting from scratch in both races.

Interviewed by the *Newark Evening News* in September 1912, Zimmerman recalled that he launched his cycling career at a race in Manasquan in the late 1880s. "I liked it so well that I jumped into the game with all the spirit that was in me," he was quoted in the September 2 feature. "I do not say this boastingly, but it seemed as if I simply couldn't lose."

In 1895, he founded the Burtis and Zimmerman Manufacturing Co., which was located on Elm Street in Freehold, according to archive notes from the Monmouth County Historical Association. From 1895 to 1900, the company manufactured several models of the "Zimmy" bicycle. In 1998, David Metz, the founder and curator of the Metz Bicycle Museum, Freehold, acquired a rare 1896 Zimmy.

Following his retirement from cycling, Zimmerman resided at 1106 Fifth Avenue in Asbury Park for more than twenty years. He died suddenly in Atlanta on October 20, 1936. His obituary in the *Times* traced his career as an amateur and professional, estimating he had won 1,400 races from 1889 to 1905.

THE EAST ORANGE FLYER

By 1900, Bloemecke had rented the Vailsburg track's operations to a group, led by Frederick W. Voigt, which looked to draw big crowds with races on Sunday afternoons. This policy violated "blue laws," community statutes designed to limit or ban commercial activities on the Sabbath. Many religious, civic and political groups were opposed the idea of Sunday cycling events. "There will be racing at Vailsburg every Sunday for the balance of the season," the *News* reported on May 5, 1900. "It is the intention of manager Voigt to continue his arrangement of programs this year."

"Many professional riders will find Newark an attractive place this summer," the *Times* wrote in its March 11, 1900 edition. Sunday racing at Vailsburg would attract top riders throughout the country, the article said.

The buzz of the 1900 season focused on a young rider from East Orange named Frank L. Kramer. Kramer, representing the Harlem Wheelmen, was the national amateur sprint champion in 1898 and 1899. He made his professional debut at Vailsburg and would go on to become one of the greatest riders of the golden era. "As an amateur last year Kramer showed as much speed as any of the professional riders and it is predicted by the racing element that Kramer will earn as worldwide a reputation as did Arthur A. Zimmerman or Eddie Bald," the *Times* wrote on March 11.

Four thousand fans were on hand for opening day at Vailsburg on Sunday afternoon, May 6, 1900. Kramer, in his first pro race, won the "inaugural half-mile dash," defeating a field that included Howard Freeman, Jay Eaton

Frank Kramer, circa 1915.
*Courtesy of Peter J. Rutledge
and George Coates Sr.*

and Bob Walthour. During his first pro season, Kramer won eighteen races and had eight second-place finishes. He finished second to Major Taylor in the national professional championship in 1900.

The 1901 season at Vailsburg opened on Decoration Day, May 30. Kramer was victorious in a half-mile contest, winning a fifty-dollar purse. Kramer captured the national championship in 1901, which began a string of sixteen consecutive titles. The designation of national champions in this era involved a system of riders earning points for first-, second- and third-place finishes throughout the season, as well as qualifying for showdown championship matches in various distance categories.

The World Almanac of Book of Facts, January 1902, posted National Cycling Association's statistics for the 1901 season. The almanac stated there were thirty-seven championship races sanctioned by the association ("the grand circuit"), which ran from July 8 to September 16, 1901. Kramer, with eighty-nine points, was the overall circuit champ, followed by Major Taylor (sixty-six points) and Iver Lawson (fifty points). Kramer also was the champion in three individual distance categories: quarter-mile, five-miles and twenty-five-miles.

Five decades before Jackie Robinson broke the color barrier in major league baseball, Marshall Walter "Major" Taylor, an African American cyclist, demonstrated his courage in the face of racism and became a world champion. Born in Indiana on November 26, 1878, he won the world one-mile cycling championship in Montreal on August 10, 1899. Taylor, who died in Chicago on June 21, 1932, passed through the Garden State during his journey as a cycling champion. Competing at Waverly on August 28, 1897, Taylor was a crowd favorite, according to the *Times*. On that day Taylor—racing out of Cambridgeport, Massachusetts—took second place in the professional mile open and won a heat in the one-mile pro handicap. Kramer placed third in the one-mile Essex County championship for amateurs.

Taylor won the one-third mile national pro championship in Asbury Park on July 27, 1898, defeating a field that included Bald and Cooper. Racing at Vailsburg on July 26, 1902, Kramer won the half-mile national pro championship race, while Taylor placed fourth.

Iver Lawson, the "Flying Swede," racing out of Salt Lake City, starred as Vailsburg opened its 1903 season on May 29. Lawson defeated Kramer in the one-mile professional Decoration Day Stakes. Newark's Bay View Wheelmen sponsored the event. Even though six thousand fans turned out for opening day, track officials expressed disappointment in the attendance figure, pointing out the lack of trolley service due to a strike had prevented an even larger audience.

A deadly fire swept through the Vailsburg board track in the early morning hours of February 16, 1904. The track had been locked up for the winter season. Newark police discovered the blaze around 1:30 a.m., and Company No. 1 was the first to respond. The fire destroyed the track's pavilion and grandstands, which measured four hundred feet long and seventy-five feet high.

The blaze claimed the life of fireman Henry Yung. The story, along with a photo of him and the twisted, charred wreckage of the bicycle track, were on page one of the February 16 edition of the *News*. He was killed when track timbers collapsed on him. Yung, who resided in Vailsburg, was thirty-five years old and had been married for eleven years to Augusta Feitzinger. He had a ten-year-old son named Harry. Yung had joined the fire department in 1896 and held the rank of sergeant of arms.

Repairs were made, and the Vailsburg track opened its 1904 season on April 10, drawing a crowd of seven thousand. Kramer received a "very flattering reception" from the crowd, the *Times* reported. He won the half-mile pro race, defeating Eddie Root of Boston, W.S. Fenn of Waterbury, Connecticut, and Joe Fogler of Brooklyn. Later that season, on August 14, Kramer won the five-mile national championship before eight thousand fans.

A crowd of only two thousand fans turned out April 2 for opening day of the 1905 season at Vailsburg. One of the reasons for the low turnout was because Frank Kramer, the main attraction, was racing in Europe. Kramer had caught the eye of Paris promoters who were eager to have the American star compete in the extensive European cycling circuit. Peter Nye wrote that Kramer captured the prestigious Grand Prix de Paris in 1905 and 1906. During his tours of Europe, Kramer won thirty-one of forty-three races.

Kramer's success against the best riders of Europe, by extension, demonstrated the world-class quality of American bicycle racing. The *Times*, in a sports roundup in its 1905 New Year's Eve edition, proclaimed in a headline that "Americans Have Figured Well in International Athletics." In addition to cycling, the article detailed the success of U.S. competitors in tennis, boxing, yacht racing, auto racing and swimming. It was a coming of age for American sports, and Kramer was an important figure in the mix.

Jackie Clarke. *Courtesy of Jeff Groman, Jazz Sport LLC.*

Racing in England, France, Germany, Holland, Belgium and Italy that season, Kramer compiled an overall record of seventeen wins and three losses.

"The year 1905 has made history in the world of international sport and is conspicuous by its brilliancy," the opening paragraph of the *Times* story declared. "The year's record shows that America more than held her own in international contests and in many branches proved to be so overwhelmingly superior she is almost invincible."

Kramer returned to the Vailsburg board track for the 1906 season. He won the featured event on September 30—a motor-pace match race, which involved three five-mile heats. W.F. Saunders was the motorcycle driver who paced Kramer. Kramer defeated James F. Moran of Chelsea, Massachusetts, who was paced by D. Connolly, winning two of the three heats.

A highlight of the 1908 season at Vailsburg came on October 25, when Kramer set a world record at twenty-five miles. The following season, Australian national champion Jackie Clarke bested Kramer's mark for twenty-five miles in a match held on October 31.

Another heralded Aussie cyclist arrived at Vailsburg in 1910. Alfred Goullet made his first appearance on Sunday, May 22, 1910, launching what would be a legendary career. Goullet, the 1909 Australian national sprint champion, attracted considerable attention from the Newark press, but his debut was disappointing—he became tangled in a fifteen-rider spill during a five-mile race.

Throughout the 1910 season, Clarke remained a tough competitor for Kramer. He defeated Kramer on October 16 in one-mile and five-mile

Jackie Clarke. *Courtesy of Jeff Groman, Jazz Sport LLC.*

matches. Then, on October 23, the last day of the season at the saucer—in what would be the final races to be held at the Vailsburg track—Clarke garnered a victory over Kramer and Lawson in a "three-corner," five-mile match. Clarke also won the five-mile open in a field that included Fogler and Root.

The Newark Velodrome

Two days after the close of Vailsburg's 1910 season, an article in the *News* would mark the next chapter of New Jersey's golden era of cycling. The story announced a new bike track was being envisioned for Newark. The lease on the Vailsburg saucer had expired on October 10. Frank M. Mihlon and John M. Chapman were working behind the scenes to build a new facility for cycling. It would be constructed opposite the Vailsburg board track, on the north side of South Orange Avenue at Munn Avenue.

The Newark Velodrome would become the crown jewel for the golden era of cycling, attracting the world's greatest racers. On March 30, 1911, the *News* reported that construction of the velodrome was on schedule, as work crews were erecting the roof over the grandstands and installing the track surface. Restless pro cyclists, training on northern New Jersey roadways throughout the month of March, were anxious to get a peek at the saucer.

Heavy rainstorms halted work on the track in early April. The *News* reported that the date originally slated to open the velodrome (April 9) would be postponed, as the grandstand roof had yet to be completed and the grounds around the saucer had turned into a "quagmire." The revised grand-opening date was set for Easter Sunday. The Newark Velodrome—a one-sixth of a mile track with a seating capacity of 12,500—opened on April 16, 1911.

"Local Bike Season Has Blustery Start" was the headline in the April 17, 1911 sports section of the *News*, which reported that the unseasonable weather conditions included high winds and snow squalls. Five thousand fans braved the chilly weather as Brooklyn's Joe Fogler was the star of the day, winning the two featured pro matches on the card: a one-mile "Eastern Handicap" and a five-mile open. Kramer had a disappointing performance, as he dropped out of the five-mile pro race at the four-mile mark, looking exhausted, according to the *Times*. Goullet placed second to Fogler in the one-mile race and finished third in the five-mile race behind Fogler and another Aussie, Paddy O'Sullivan Hehir.

Riders take a spin at Newark Velodrome, which was still under construction, in April 1911. *Courtesy of Jeff Groman, Jazz Sport LLC.*

"The accommodations are ideal and the manner of handling the crowd is all that could be expected," the *News* reported, as fans gave the track rave reviews. The new velodrome was hailed as "the most-complete track" in the United States, as every seat offered an unobstructed view.

In appreciation of the track's impressive workmanship, the opening ceremonies honored construction crews with flowers, as fans saluted them with applause. Mihlon received two floral horseshoes and a floral bicycle, while Chapman was given a good-luck horseshoe piece. The two owners were lavished with additional flowers from the bike riders, track officials and business associates.

Competition in Newark was fierce and each week new story lines and subplots emerged. Fogler, on Sunday, April 23, captured the two-mile pro race, the featured event of the day. Once again, he got the better of Kramer. "Whatever national champion Frank Kramer has done to Joe Fogler on a bicycle track in past competitions will be lost sight of in the figuring out of possibilities for the future, should the Brooklyn speed merchant continue the sensational riding he has shown so far at the local velodrome," the April 24 feature in the *News* stated. "Fogler has all the speed in the world. He took the champion's measure…something never dreamed of and in such a

Joe Fogler. *Courtesy of Jeff Groman, Jazz Sport LLC.*

manner that a new alignment of championship possibilities for 1911 will be necessary." Though he lost the two-mile match, Kramer did prevail in the half-mile handicap.

The commentary regarding Kramer's demise proved to be a bit premature, as he won the three-mile pro open "in sensational style" on May 7. Fogler was second, followed by Hehir, Fred Hill of Boston and John Bedell of Newark.

Races at the Newark Velodrome were festive events. The *News*, in its May 8 edition, reported:

> *Cycle racing's popularity in Newark was never better illustrated than at the Velodrome yesterday afternoon, when an unprecedented crowd of 12,000 packed into the grandstand and bleachers and overflowed into the infield to witness the weekly card of contests…There was every conceivable brand of enthusiast, from old men down through the middle aged and youths to boys and girls and even babies in arms. The whole presented a great sight in the*

Newark Velodrome's ticket window. Note the diverse assortment of hats worn by virtually every member of the crowd. *Courtesy of Jeff Groman, Jazz Sport LLC.*

amphitheater-like stands and with the bright colors of women's gowns and millinery it made a spectacle that has never been surpassed at a sporting event in this vicinity.

The Newark Velodrome's inaugural season closed on October 29, with Kramer winning the one-mile pro open, defeating Clarke and Root.

The 1912 World Championship

The Newark Velodrome's second season would see Frank Kramer crowned as a world champion. He began the campaign in fine form on opening day, April 21, when he took first place in the two-mile pro open match, defeating Leon Comes of Paris and Fogler. The season also would see the arrival of yet another great Australian champion—the Tasmanian, Alfred Grenda. Like Clarke and Goullet, Grenda quickly emerged as a strong challenger to Kramer. Grinding duels between Grenda and Kramer during the 1912 season would presage the world championship. Grenda established himself as a powerful racer before eight thousand fans on May 27, first by winning the Australian pursuit race,

51

overtaking Peter A. Drobach of Boston, and then by beating Kramer and Newark cyclist Frank Cavanagh in the five-mile pro open race.

Nye, in an article written for the U.S. Bicycling Hall of Fame, explained that Chapman drew on his international contacts to have the world championships held in Newark. Union Cycliste Internationale, the sport's international governing body, would sanction the competition. Racers from as many countries as those who went to the Stockholm Olympics that summer converged on Newark. The *Times*, in a February 6, 1910 report, stated that Chapman, in late January of that year, had filed an application with the National Cycling Association's board of control for the world championship. The application was to be considered by the association and then passed along to Union Cycliste Internationale.

A series of qualifying races began in Newark on June 2, 1912. Kramer won the quarter-mile national championship, and Grenda was victorious in the three-mile handicap. Kramer and John Bedell captured the one-mile pro team match race July 1 before 5,500 fans, defeating the teams of Grenda and Drobach and Comes and Cavanaugh. However, Grenda prevailed in the five-mile pro open race, defeating Comes and Kramer. Four days later, Kramer nipped Grenda and Bedell in the five-mile pro Spartan Stakes.

Newark Velodrome's parking lot. Note the South Orange Avenue trolley cars in the distance. *Courtesy of Jeff Groman, Jazz Sport LLC.*

Drobach won the five-mile national championship at the Newark Velodrome on July 4, outpacing a field that included Kramer and Grenda.

The competition between Grenda and Kramer further intensified on July 8 in a one-mile match race, billed as a showdown between the Australian and American champions. Kramer rose to the occasion, defeating Grenda in consecutive heats. Later, in a two-mile pro handicap, Kramer once again topped Grenda. The rivalry kept rolling throughout the midsummer weeks, as a crowd of eight thousand cheered on August 4 when Kramer bested Grenda and Marcel Dupuy of France in a one-mile "grand-prize" match. The prize was a $500 purse.

Kramer defeated Emil Friol of France in one-mile match races (winning two of three heats) on August 7 and again on August 11. Friol was touted as the "greatest rider in Europe." Though the two had comparable speed, the *News* cited Kramer's masterful track tactics as being the decisive factor in the races.

The world professional sprint championship came down to a one-mile event to determine the world's fastest rider. The final match was slated for Sunday, September 1, but it was postponed because of rain and held the next day. The championship featured three world-class athletes: Kramer, the U.S. hero; Grenda, the top cyclist of Australia; and André Perchicot, the champion of France. Each man won a qualifying heat against other riders to reach the final. In the end, it was Kramer who prevailed.

The *News'* headline in its Tuesday, September 3 edition proclaimed Kramer had crowned his "wonderful career" by winning the world championship. It was a thrilling competition, as inches separated the three riders at the finish line. Kramer, positioned in

Frank Kramer, adorned with flowers, following his 1912 world championship victory at the Newark Velodrome. *Courtesy of Jeff Groman, Jazz Sport LLC.*

the center of the track, beat Grenda by a foot, with Perchicot in the third spot. Grenda was leading at the final turn, but Kramer's sprint was decisive in the home stretch.

Kramer was treated to "a demonstration worthy of his victory," the September 3 article stated.

While still mounted on his wheel, he was decorated with the world's championship sash by Richard F. Kelsey, chairman of the National Cycling Association. A wreath of flowers was placed on his shoulders and a bouquet was thrust into his hands. The band played the Star Spangled Banner, the crowd yelled and cheered. Kramer bowed and smiled and made a triumphant tour around the track. Later, a crowd waited outside the velodrome until Kramer appeared in street attire and cheered him and demanded a speech. The champion, modest to a degree and especially short on speechmaking, hurried to his motor car and, still all smiles, waved his hat to the throng.

"Albert" (Alf) Francis Grenda, dubbed the "Tall Tasmanian" (a strapping man over six feet tall), was one of eight children of German-born parents,

according to the Australian Dictionary of Biography. Born September 15, 1889, he came to the United States under contract to compete in the 1912 season. Grenda and Goullet are famously associated as the winning teammates of the November 1914 six-day race at Madison Square Garden, when they rode a record 2,759.2 miles. The two racers also won six-day races in Boston in 1916 and again in New York in 1923. Grenda retired from cycling in 1926, moved to California and became an American citizen in 1930. He died May 30, 1977, in Paradise, California.

Alf Grenda. *Courtesy of Jeff Groman, Jazz Sport LLC.*

THE OUTLAW SEASON

News reports estimated the Newark Velodrome grossed more than $200,000 in its first season and had similar success in 1912, highlighted by the world championship. But a rival operation known as the Newark Motordrome—a quarter-mile track specially designed for motorcycling racing, owned by Inglis Moore Uppercu, an automotive tycoon—challenged the velodrome's franchise. The motordrome was built across the street from the Newark Velodrome, on the south side of South Orange Avenue, overlapping the area where the Vailsburg board track had been located. Eager to witness the high-speed racing, eight thousand fans turned out as the motordrome opened on July 4, 1912.

The motordrome was the site of a horrific accident on Sunday, September 8, 1912, when two motorcycle riders, Eddie Hasha and Johnny Albright, crashed into the bleachers, killing themselves and five spectators and injuring more than a dozen. A sixth spectator died one day later at Newark City Hospital. The incident made the front pages of the *Newark Evening News* and the *New York Times*.

In the wake of this tragedy, a series of parallel events unfolded during the 1913 season, as detailed by Nye. Uppercu made plans to hold bicycle races at the motordrome (Newark had banned motorcycle races immediately following the September 8 accident). Chapman's abrasive, heavy-handed management style was wearing thin on bike riders. Mihlon, whose family owned the lucrative Long Bar Saloon in Newark, was reassessing his financial portfolio and near-term business strategies.

Biding his time was Floyd MacFarland, the veteran cyclist who had distinguished himself as the manager of the Salt Palace, Salt Lake City, during the 1912 season and put together a successful tour of races in Europe in early 1913. Born in San Jose, California, and later residing in Virginia, MacFarland began his racing career in 1893. Best known as a six-day rider, his journey as a professional carried him to Europe, Australia and throughout North America. His racing career ended in New Haven, Connecticut, in 1911.

Eager to advance his career as a promoter and manager, MacFarland had his eye on the prize: the Newark saucer. For a period, bicycle races were held at the velodrome and the motordrome. By the middle of the 1913 season, MacFarland seized upon the chance to serve as intermediary between Uppercu and Mihlon.

"MacFarland strategy was opportunistic," Nye wrote. "He brought the two track owners together. He recommended that Mihlon let Uppercu

Floyd MacFarland, 1910. *Courtesy of Jeff Groman, Jazz Sport LLC.*

buy a half interest in the Newark Velodrome in exchange for Uppercu's closing the (motordrome)." Mihlon "graciously agreed" to the proposal, and the new business associates, in turn, decided to hire MacFarland to manage the Newark track—in effect, ousting Chapman. The move also had an impact outside the Garden State, as Newark was part of a circuit that included tracks in New Haven and Boston.

The *Times*, on August 2, 1913, spelled out terms of the pact. The "warring factions" of Newark merged and conciliated. Henry Amerman, Uppercu's attorney, formally confirmed the deal on August 1 from his New York office in the Woolworth Building.

The *Times* reported:

> *Uppercu and Frank Mihlon are the big figures in the new combine, with Patrick T. Powers and Floyd MacFarland also interested…The company, to be known as the Cycle Racing Association, a New Jersey corporation, will hold its first meeting on Monday afternoon [August 4], when officers will be elected. John M. Chapman, who was Mihlon's partner in conducting races at the velodrome races, sold out his interests. Chapman was not in favor of the merger, considering Uppercu and the men who backed him in starting the Motordrome as "outlaws" to the sport.*

The article credited Chapman's achievements, who, since 1908 (when he came to Newark to manage the Vailsburg board track), "put the sport, which had been dwindling, on a paying basis." The story also confirmed that MacFarland would succeed Chapman as manager of the Newark Velodrome.

"John Chapman was one of the greatest sports promoters who ever lived," Carmine Bilotti, a veteran sports promoter and public relations director, said in an interview in the early 1980s. Bilotti worked as Chapman's assistant during the Newark Velodrome's final years of operation. "Chapman had his share of enemies, but he turned bicycle racing into a major spectator sport."

The *Times*, in its August 3, 1913 edition, reported the Newark Velodrome riders were "incensed at Frank Mihlon...for making a truce with the Motormen without consulting the riders about it." The situation escalated into a labor dispute, and riders huddled into rival camps—the velodrome cyclists and the Motordrome "outlaws." Cyclists who had crossed South Orange Avenue to compete at the motordrome, in effect, broke away from the National Cycling Association (NCA), the sport's governing body, and the velodrome bike riders were opposed to their reinstatement. The article said Richard F. Kelsey, the NCA chairman, received a formal protest against the outlaw riders.

There was big money at stake in the outlaw controversy. The *Times*, on November 1, 1914, reported that $86,000 was paid out to cyclists during the 1914 outdoor season. Frank Kramer was the highest-paid rider, drawing $10,511, followed by German rider Walter Rutt ($5,976) and Alf Goullet ($5,122).

The outlaw situation continued to simmer in the following years. The *Times* reported on April 4, 1916, that the recently organized Federation of American Cyclists had aligned itself with the Essex Trades Council, a labor union. The council filed an "unfair labor" protest against the Newark Velodrome and the NCA. Mihlon and Uppercu dismissed the protest, issuing a statement that the "Essex Trades Council has exceeded its authority. Athletics and organized labor have nothing in common...never before has there ever been an attempt to place any sport under the jurisdiction of organized labor." For its part, the Federation of American Cyclists charged that race promoters controlled the NCA. "The riders want an open market in which to dispose of their services. The promoters want a closed market."

A "Dominant, Aggressive Figure"

Floyd MacFarland was at the helm of the Newark Velodrome at the start of the 1914 season, and the track's business blossomed under his guidance. "MacFarland became the premier cycling promoter of competitive cycling in America," Nye wrote. He had a "golden touch" in managing various bicycling events, "for success after success came of his ventures. Everyone seemed to win, for the sport's popularity enhanced the lesser promoters and a majority of the riders." Meanwhile, the *Times* reported on February 25, 1914, that Chapman, speaking from his home in Atlanta, said he "was through with the bicycle game."

MacFarland laid out ambitious plans for the 1915 season, which included world championship races in Newark, Boston and Philadelphia. He created a velodrome in Chicago, which was slated to open in May of that year, and had decided to extend the cycling circuit with a velodrome in Toronto, which he had tapped Chapman to manage.

On the afternoon of April 17, 1915, just prior to the start of the season, MacFarland became embroiled in a heated argument outside the velodrome with a Brooklyn concessionaire named David Lantenberg. The two men started to fight, and during the melee, MacFarland was stabbed with a screwdriver behind his left ear and collapsed. He was rushed to Newark City Hospital, where he died at 9:00 p.m., never regaining consciousness, the *Times* reported. Mihlon, Kramer and MacFarland's wife were at his bedside. He would have been thirty-nine years old on July 9. At the time of his death, MacFarland and his wife resided in Newark at 73 North Munn Avenue, a short walk from the velodrome. His funeral was held April 21, and he was buried in Buffalo, New York.

Chapman had made plans to travel to Toronto, but Mihlon and Uppercu reconnected with him and persuaded him to return to Newark. On April 23, 1915, the *Times* reported that Chapman was coming back to Newark.

Newark police arrested Lantenberg and held him at the city's Seventh Police Station. The charges against him shifted to manslaughter from assault. Eventually, he was acquitted of all charges on June 23, Nye reported.

As a eulogy to MacFarland, the *Times* on April 25, 1915, wrote:

> *Cycledom lost its most dominant and aggressive figure and the man who, more than anyone else, stamped his personality on the sport…MacFarland's genius as a racing manager consisted of his ability to give the sport an almost unending series of novel ideas. He devised new races and new tests of skill on the bicycle and he could match the riders in such a way as to provide the most interesting competition.*

Sixty-five years later, Goullet still lamented the loss of MacFarland, expressing admiration for his friend's vision and leadership.

Chapter 3

REQUIEM FOR TWO HEAVYWEIGHTS

"I MUST BOW TO FATHER TIME"

While the loss of MacFarland overshadowed the 1915 season, it also was a time to step back and celebrate Frank Kramer's amazing career. The *Times*, in an April 18, 1915 article, citing an inventory of records kept by Kramer himself, reported that the champ had registered 646 victories (77 of which came when he was an amateur) over eighteen seasons.

Born November 21, 1880, in Evansville, Indiana, Kramer—nicknamed "Big Steve"—was a longtime resident of East Orange. Various accounts suggested Kramer had health problems as a child. The U.S. Bicycling Hall of Fame inducted Kramer in 1988 and underlined his many achievements. He won sixteen consecutive national pro sprint championships from 1901 to 1916. His string of U.S. championships was broken in 1917, but he regained the crown in 1918 and again in 1921.

The forty-year-old Kramer came out flying in 1921, opening the season at the Newark Velodrome on March 27 by winning the (Newark) Mayor Charles P. Gillen Stakes, a five-mile race, defeating Peter Moeskops of the Netherlands, Reggie McNamara and Alf Goullet. One week later, he again bested the same three riders in another five-mile match and then rode with Italian rider Orlando Piani to win the one-mile team race, defeating the combo of Moeskops and Goullet. On April 24, sixteen thousand fans watched as he topped Willie Spencer of Toronto and Walter Rutt in a three-corner, one-mile match race.

However, after many miles of competition, the long ride for Kramer came to an end on July 26, 1922. The lead sports story in the Monday, July 24, 1922 edition of the *Newark Evening News* carried the headline: "Kramer Announces Retirement as Cyclist, Will Ride Farewell Race Wednesday Night." To the left of the headline was a three-column drawing, which depicted the lantern-jawed Kramer handing over his crown to a bearded, bespectacled Father Time, seated at his desk with a writing quill in hand. "I'm through!" the Kramer character tersely declared in his word balloon.

According to the article, Kramer walked into John Chapman's office on July 23 following his team victory with Ray Eaton, the 1919 national pro champ, to say he had just ridden his final race. Kramer told the *News* that his decision was due to health concerns, and that he had contemplated the move for some time. He was under a physician's care since the start of the 1922 season. Medical examinations showed that, aside from the physical wear and tear on his body, his nervous system had been worn threadbare due to the long years of intensive training and the stress from competition. The strain of racing had taken its toll, and he reached a point where he no longer was able to sleep.

Seven years before the 1922 season, Kramer had pondered the possibility of leaving the cycling game. An article in the August 10, 1915 edition of the *Times* speculated that the champion was considering retirement:

> *He admits that he has apparently reached the end of this racing career. Kramer has about $200,000 invested in first-mortgage bonds, all earned by his cycling. During the racing seasons of 1906, 1907, 1913 and 1914 Kramer defeated all rivals in Europe. In 1906 and 1907 he won the Grand Prix of Paris, worth $2,500 to the winner. His appearance in European races attracted record crowds at tracks in Paris, Berlin, Brussels, Copenhagen and other capitals. Every season he receives a bonus of $7,500 for riding exclusively on the tracks of the Cycle Racing Association at Newark, Boston, Philadelphia, Sheepshead Bay [New York], Chicago and Toronto. All prize money won by the champion, never less than $5,000 a season, makes his income about $12,500. Kramer's season on European tracks netted him $5,000, his contracts stipulating that sum with all expenses.*

He bid adieu to cycling fans at two separate venues on consecutive nights. His first goodbye was staged at the New York Velodrome on July 25, 1922. The *Times* recorded the event in its July 26, 1922 edition, writing that Kramer would "never forget the thunderous ovation he received from 8,000 fans that braved the threatening weather to see the East Orange marvel ride."

Following his appearance in New York, the stage was set for Kramer's farewell in Newark. "Bicycle fans of the present day and years gone by are expected to be on hand (tonight) to help give the retiring champion one of the greatest ovations he has ever received," the July 26 story in the *News* reported.

Kramer's stated goal was to beat the mark for one-sixth of a mile. A rider out of Salt Lake City named Musty Crebs held the record, a time of fifteen and two-fifths seconds. Kramer's personal-best time for the lap was fifteen and four-fifths seconds. He was unsuccessful in his attempt at the mark during his farewell appearance at the New York Velodrome. Just as he did at the New York track, Alf Grenda would pace Kramer for his try at the record in Newark.

A sports commentary in the July 26 edition of the *News* laid out the drama that was about to unfold:

Frank Kramer, his final appearance at the Newark Velodrome, July 26, 1922, with trainer Maury Gordon. *Courtesy of Jeff Groman, Jazz Sport LLC.*

They're bidding farewell to Frank Kramer tonight at the [Newark] Velodrome. Tonight Kramer will write "finis" to one of the greatest athletic careers the world has ever known. Sure enough, there'll be tense moments on the hill [the Newark saucer] tonight; tense moments and perchance a damp eye here and there, for cycle fandom is as quick as any to recognize the fair and the square. Recognizing this, all bikedom knows full well that when the broad back of Kramer is turned tonight on the grandstand in his last march to the dressing room as an active competitor, when the sturdy-spoken steed is hung high to gather dust and cobwebs in shadows and quiet of an East Orange attic, cycling will have seen the last of a champion who has played his game long and played it hard, but played it square at every turn.

In his last spin on the Newark saucer, he equaled the record for a sixth of a mile. Three timers were on hand that night, as requested by Kramer, to accurately document his attempt at the record. "The great old rider was speeding at this best," the *Newark Evening News* reported in its July 27, 1922 edition. "It was a beautiful sight to see the East Orange flyer's legs work with their old snap and drive, with the same old precision that carried him through so many strenuous years of campaigning."

Track announcer Willie Sullivan told the hushed crowd that Kramer had equaled the time for the distance, the story continued, and a "mighty cheer went up. The tribute Kramer received as he rode around the track on his tour of honor, wrapped in Old Glory, is one that will long be remembered."

A two-column headline on page one of the same edition read: "Kramer Is Glorious Victor in Last Race, Against Time." The story spared no expense in vividly describing the dramatic spectacle:

Night and light and colors in a huge wooden bowl! Fifteen thousand persons hoarse with cheering. Women smiling as tears misted their eyes and men grinning and trying to keep down lumps in their throats. Never before has Newark witnessed such a spectacle. It was election night, the World Series and Armistice Day all in one.

Dressed in black trunks and a white silk shirt, Kramer smiled at the crowd, but then the moment suddenly "gripped him," and his mood turned solemn. He was, the article observed, a solitary figure on the rim of the track, realizing he had reached the end of a long journey.

"I want to thank you for the interest you have shown in me and your appreciation of my efforts," Kramer said to the fans, using the announcer's microphone. "I have done my best for 26 years. I am sorry I am not 15 years younger. However, I have no alternative and must bow to Father Time."

The celebration lasted for thirty minutes, a heartfelt tribute reminiscent of the outpouring of emotion from the fans when Kramer won the world championship at the Newark track in 1912.

The Saturday following Kramer's final bow at the Newark Velodrome, the *News* ran a four-column illustration titled "Who's the Cinderella?" The drawing depicted a semicircle of perplexed-looking racers surrounding a giant pair of Kramer's empty racing shoes. The symbolism was clear: who would be the next rider great enough to take Kramer's place? The question would prove prophetic to the sport's fate in the years ahead.

"With Frank Kramer gone, there's a void to be filled and the principal asset for the aspirant for the job of supplanting Kramer is popularity," the *News* sports commentary, which ran below the illustration, stated in the July 29, 1922 edition. "It was Kramer's popularity as much as his speed that kept cycling alive here."

Following his retirement, Kramer remained active in cycling. He was appointed chairman of the board of control of the National Cycling Association and served as a referee at the Newark, New York and Nutley Velodromes. He also was president of the Wooden Legs, a social club for retired professional cyclists, which sponsored annual dinners in Newark.

The Newark Velodrome, May 13, 1929. *Courtesy of the Newark Public Library.*

Outside of the bicycle game, Kramer was a member of the East Orange Police Commission and was active in the Boy Scouts of America.

Kramer had inherited his athletic ability from his father, Louis Kramer, who competed internationally in gymnastics, wrestling and fencing. As a youth, Frank Kramer was sent to live with Dillon B. Burnett of East Orange, who was a partner in Louis Kramer's furniture manufacturing business. Kramer's parents, apparently due to concerns for their son's health, decided the northern New Jersey climate would be more beneficial compared to the midwestern air in Evansville.

He first was attracted to bicycle racing in the mid-1890s. At the time he was a student at South Eighth Street School in East Orange. Among his highlights as an amateur, Kramer, in 1898, won the half-mile match at the National Cycledrome at Ambrose Park in Brooklyn on May 28; captured the one-mile race at Asbury Park on July 27; and won the New Jersey one-mile amateur state championship at Vailsburg on August 20. In 1899, he won on June 24 the one-mile race at Brooklyn's Manhattan Beach Cycle Track (a concrete oval) and then returned to the cycledrome on July 1 and won the quarter-mile dash.

Frank Louis Kramer died of a heart attack in his sleep on the morning of Wednesday, October 8, 1958, at Orange Memorial Hospital. He had entered the hospital on September 25. At the time of his death, he resided at 61 Park End Place in East Orange and was survived by his wife, Helen Hay Kramer. He was buried at Rosedale Cemetery, Orange

Willie Ratner wrote a remembrance article in the October 10, 1958 edition of the *News*:

Frank Kramer's grave, Rosedale Cemetery, Orange. *Courtesy of M. Gabriele.*

Requiem for Two Heavyweights

To watch Kramer ride was like watching Bobby Jones play golf, Jack Dempsey in action or Babe Ruth at bat. He had that thing called "class," which comes naturally to some athletes, but which others couldn't develop in a thousand years. A man must be born with it and Kramer surely was, for he was a star from the first to the last day that he straddled his bike."

However, Ratner knew there was a price Kramer had paid for his intense dedication to the sport. He was, according to Ratner, a "strange man" with numerous eccentricities:

He never fraternized with bike riders and had only a few intimate friends. He was always in bed by 9 o'clock during his riding days and was so punctual in this respect that neighbors could set their clocks when the lights in Kramer's room went out. Since he allowed so few people to get close to him, he was a hard man to know, except for his life and exploits on the track.

During his final years of competition, Kramer often was the victim of harsh criticism from the fans and press, as he no longer was able to live up to his own lofty standards. In the privacy of the dressing room following those races, Kramer confessed to being deeply hurt by this treatment, Ratner recalled.

"Twenty-five years a racing cyclist and every year on top is the story of Frank L. Kramer," Ratner wrote. "So long, Steve."

The Young Man from Emu

A reporter from the *New York Times* visited cycling legend Alfred Timothy Goullet in February 1973 at his Newark home. The *Times* article—"The Iron Man at 82," published on February 28, 1973—discussed Goullet's prolific career, an international resume that included more than four hundred wins and fifteen six-day race victories. Goullet was voted into the U.S. Bicycling Hall of Fame (in 1988, the same year as Kramer); the Sport Australia Hall of Fame; the Madison Square Garden Hall of Fame; and the New York Sports Hall of Fame.

Born April 5, 1891, Goullet and his family lived in Emu, in the state of Victoria, Australia. Growing up near Sydney and Melbourne, Goullet was captivated by cycling. He entered amateur races at age seventeen and became the Australian national sprint champion in 1909. During numerous conversations in the 1980s, Goullet said that, as an aspiring cyclist, it was an

American, Floyd MacFarland, who became his hero. MacFarland raced in Australia during the 1901–1904 seasons.

"I used to read about Major Taylor, Iver Lawson and Floyd MacFarland," Goullet said in the *Times* interview, recalling his formative years. "When I finally got a peek at MacFarland in Australia, he struck my fancy. I followed him wherever he went on the streets." In years to come, after Goullet landed in the United States, the two reconnected and forged a friendship. They also briefly became competitors. MacFarland, during his final race, in New Haven, Connecticut, in 1911, won a ten-mile motor-pace event, riding against a field that included Goullet.

In 1910, Goullet packed his bags and boarded a boat to the United States, wanting to race in Newark, which he called "the center of racing in America." He disembarked from an ocean liner in the middle of a March blizzard wearing a straw hat. He was one of many noteworthy riders imported from Australia and New Zealand to race in Newark, a roster that included Grenda, Jackie Clarke, Robert Spears, Cecil Walker, Reggie McNamara and Paddy O'Sullivan Hehir.

Alf Goullet. *Courtesy of Jeff Groman, Jazz Sport LLC.*

Goullet confessed to being overwhelmed and discouraged by the competition he initially encountered at the Vailsburg track. His recollection wasn't false modesty. He indeed got off to a slow start in Newark during the 1910 season, unable to shake off the "sea legs" from his long voyage, the *News* wrote. He also was a victim of bad luck. In his debut at Vailsburg track on May 22, he crashed along with fourteen other riders.

"I was a failure at the start and was about to return home when

Joe Fogler (the Brooklyn cyclist) encouraged me to stay, for which I was thankful," he told the *Times*.

He competed in various events during the next three weeks, gaining plaudits from sports writers, even though he was unable to win a race. Finally, he broke through with his first victory on June 19, 1910, defeating Percy Lawrence of San Francisco in an Unlimited Australian Match Pursuit Race. The win sparked his confidence, and he defeated Kramer in the same pursuit format on June 26 and July 17. He again won a pursuit match on July 24, beating his chum Fogler. Goullet continued to gain traction throughout the summer, and he topped Eddie Root on September 4 in a ten-mile pursuit race.

When the season ended at Vailsburg, Goullet went to Madison Square Garden for the start of the indoor circuit. On December 3, 1910 he was one of eighteen riders to compete in a ten-mile race for professionals, a match won by Fogler. Goullet then paired with Hehir as the "Kangaroo Team" in the Garden's featured six-day race and they finished fourth.

For the 1912 season, Goullet traveled to the Salt Palace Velodrome in Salt Lake City, reuniting with MacFarland, who served there as track manager. Wire service reports published in the *Newark Evening News* indicated Goullet was a rising star, as he won an assortment of sprint and distance events. Goullet faced stiff competition in Salt Lake City, riding against Fogler, Clarke, Root, Hehir and Lawson.

Goullet and the other riders came back to Newark for the start of the 1913 season. They joined Kramer, who had returned to New Jersey in early April after a successful tour of races in France and Germany. On opening day, April 20, Goullet captured the one-mile pro handicap match.

June 8, 1913, marked a stellar performance by Goullet at the

Alf Goullet. *Courtesy of Jeff Groman, Jazz Sport LLC.*

Newark track, when he won the one-mile national championship, defeating Clarke, Fogler and Kramer; the one-mile handicap, beating a field that included Grenda; and the three-mile open, again outdistancing Clarke, Fogler and Kramer.

Goullet accumulated U.S. track titles as the decade unfolded. He captured the two-mile national pro championship on July 18, 1915, defeating Kramer. He won the five-mile national pro championship—on July 18, 1914 (at New York's Brighton Beach Motordrome), and on September 6, 1915, and July 8, 1917 (both at Newark)—finishing ahead of Kramer in all three of the five-mile victories.

In mid-December 1917, one week after winning a six-day race with Jake Magin at Madison Square Garden, Goullet enlisted in the navy, joining the Aviation Corps to support the U.S. war effort. One year earlier, he had become an American citizen. He was stationed in Pensacola, Florida, for eight months.

He rejoined the Newark circuit for the start of the 1919 season, winning the five-mile Mayor Charles P. Gillen stakes on April 6, defeating Kramer and others. Kramer came back to beat Goullet in the five-mile national championship on September 14, 1919, further fueling their rivalry.

Fans and competitors recognized Goullet had a rare combination of world-class cycling skills; he was a formidable rider in long-distance and sprint events. He showcased this ability in Newark on June 5, 1921. He defeated William J. Bailey, the English cycling champ, in a one-mile match race and then overpowered Walker, Grenda and Peter Drobach to win the ten-mile open.

By 1921, press reports in the *Times* frequently identified Goullet as "America's premier cyclist," "the all-around bicycle champion of America" and "the greatest all-around bicycle rider in the world." He was a headliner at Newark, as well as Madison Square Garden and the New York Velodrome, located on 225th Street and Broadway, which opened May 30, 1922. A highlight of his 1922 season came on June 29, when he defeated Kramer, Willie Spencer and Italian star Orlando Piani in Newark to take the two-mile national championship.

On March 10, 1923, Goullet, paired with Grenda, won his eighth and final six-day race at Madison Square Garden. The two had captured the Garden's six-day marathon in 1914 when they combined to clock 2,759 miles and one lap. The 1923 competition, which ended at 11:00 p.m., had a dramatic finish as the "two old masters" put together a "supreme effort" of late sprints, edging the team of Sammy Gastman and Dave Landis, according

NEW YORK VELODROME

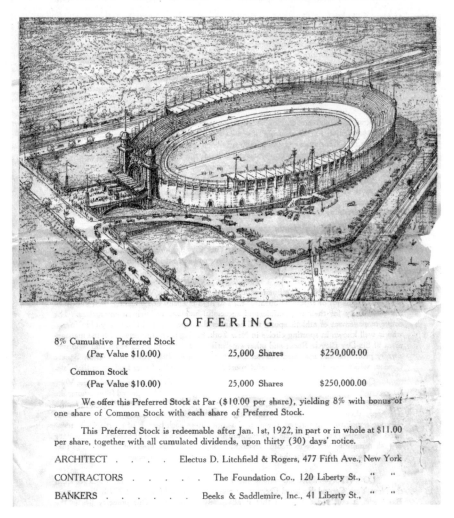

OFFERING

8% Cumulative Preferred Stock
(Par Value $10.00)   25,000 Shares $250,000.00

Common Stock
(Par Value $10.00)   25,000 Shares $250,000.00

We offer this Preferred Stock at Par ($10.00 per share), yielding 8% with bonus of one share of Common Stock with each share of Preferred Stock.

This Preferred Stock is redeemable after Jan. 1st, 1922, in part or in whole at $11.00 per share, together with all cumulated dividends, upon thirty (30) days' notice.

ARCHITECT . . . . Electus D. Litchfield & Rogers, 477 Fifth Ave., New York

CONTRACTORS . . . . . The Foundation Co., 120 Liberty St., " "

BANKERS . . . . . . Beeks & Saddlemire, Inc., 41 Liberty St., " "

Cover page, investment prospectus for the New York Velodrome. *Courtesy of Otto Eisele.*

to coverage in the March 11, 1923 edition of the *Times*. Peter Van Kempen of the Netherlands and his Swiss teammate, Oscar Egg, finished third.

It would be the last hurrah for Goullet in his signature event. The *Times* wrote that fifteen thousand raucous fans, flinging their hats and coats into the air, gave the winning team a spirited ovation.

It was a happy moment for Goullet who, despite his usual high esteem by the bike fans, found himself booed daily by the fickle crowd, especially when Peter Van Kempen, the young Holland meteor, defeated him in the sprints on innumerable occasions during the week. It was an especially notable triumph in the view of the fact that, after competing in the six-day grind at Chicago less than a month ago, he was confined to his bed for 10 days with an attack of influenza and competed in the present grind against the advice of his friends and his physician.

During the 1924 season, Goullet twice defeated Arthur Spencer in two-mile match races, on May 18 in Newark and June 3 at the New York Velodrome. Spencer, a robust 220-pound rider from Toronto, had dethroned Kramer as U.S. professional champ in 1917 and 1920. Goullet lost to Peter Moeskops of the Netherlands, the reigning world cycling champion, in a one-mile match race in Newark on August 20, 1924.

Goullet suffered a setback on December 13, 1924 when, competing in the fifth day of a six-day race at the Garden, he was rushed to New York Hospital with an attack of appendicitis. Following surgery, he spent two weeks recuperating at the hospital. The *Times* reported on December 27, 1924, that Goullet was going to marry Jane Rooney of Newark on January 5, 1925, and the couple planned a honeymoon trip to Europe.

Returning to New Jersey after his European excursion, Goullet was on hand for the Newark Velodrome's opening day, April 5, 1925, winning the one-mile handicap. Still feeling the effects of his surgery, he won a one-mile match race against Cecil Walker on May 10. The highlight of Goullet's 1925 campaign in Newark came on September 5 when he set a new world record for twenty-five miles on a track. The *Times* reported he broke the old mark held by Grenda, which was set at the Newark saucer four years earlier.

Following the conclusion of the Newark Velodrome's 1925 season, Goullet signed for $10,000 to compete at Madison Square Garden's six-day race, which began on November 29. The results, however, were disappointing. "It is doubtful if the old master of the wheel (Goullet) will even try to improve the position which he and Cecil Walker are occupying—nine laps in arrears," the *Times* reported on December 4, 1925.

After sitting out the next season at Newark, Goullet's final appearance as a professional cyclist came in December 1926, when he and American sprint champion Freddie Spencer teamed up for the forty-first international six-day race at Madison Square Garden. Action at the Garden on the opening evening of December 4, 1926, confirmed Goullet's illustrious career had come to an end. Ten thousand fans turned out for preliminary events to kick off the grind, as Franco Georgetti of Italy—an Olympian and respected champion during the 1920s—easily outdistanced Goullet in the one-mile match race.

"Georgetti proved himself the veteran's master," the *Times* observed in its December 5, 1926 edition. "At no time was the New Jersey star (Goullet)... able to cope with the speed that Georgetti commanded." The *Times*, on December 11, 1926, reported the Goullet/Spencer team was in last place, eighteen laps off the pace.

During his later years, Goullet continued to live in the Newark area, enjoying his status as an elder statesman of the bicycling game, ever dapper in a suit, tie and hat. He died at a nursing home in Toms River on March 11, 1995, just shy of his 104th birthday.

In retrospect, Fogler's friendly intervention in 1910 persuaded a disheartened Goullet to stay the course and live out what was to be his legendary career. It also sparked a successful partnership, as the two riders, in 1913, teamed to win six-day races in Paris (on January 19) and New York

The Newark Velodrome, 1925. *Courtesy of Jeff Groman, Jazz Sport LLC.*

Joe Fogler (seated) and Alf Goullet, dressed to the nines. *Courtesy of Jeff Groman, Jazz Sport LLC.*

(on December 13). Fogler won four additional six-day races at Madison Square Garden with other partners.

According to Social Security and U.S. census records, Fogler was born on March 17, 1884, in Brooklyn and died in January 1970. He began his amateur career in 1903, and among his first competitions, placed second on May 30, 1903, in a two-mile race at Vailsburg and took second on August 1, 1903, in a half-mile race at Manhattan Beach track. He turned pro in 1904 and became a fixture at the Vailsburg saucer and the Newark Velodrome.

Fogler retired in 1915, and the following season, he was signed to manage bicycle meets in Chicago. By 1920, he served as a director of six-day races at Madison Square Garden. In one of his final appearances in the cycling game, the *Times* reported Fogler was chief referee at a "revival" six-day race at New York's 102nd Engineers Armory, located at Fort Washington Avenue and 168th Street, which began on March 22, 1959.

Chapter 4

CYCLING COMES TO NUTLEY

THE DOWNHILL TREND

A story in the *Newark Evening News*, on April 1, 1926, carried this sarcastic headline: "Colonel Chapman Will Comb Europe for Fast Bike Talent." An unflattering drawing of Chapman, bundled in an overcoat, doffing his hat, illustrated he was on his way across the Atlantic:

> *As fast as the Berengaria* [an ocean liner built in 1912] *can carry him, Colonel Chapman is dashing for Europe. The cold, astute colonel is being accompanied by Frank Mihlon. No one who knows the colonel will believe that the little Napoleon of bike racing would go beyond hearing the velodrome turnstiles just as the season is to open unless it was urgent. And you don't have to have your palm read to learn why it's urgent. With baseball returning to Newark by popular subscription, the colonel sees the business of bike racing about to meet up with an active competitor...the colonel is going to meet it with the swiftest prima donnas on French bike tracks and the fastest yodelers in Switzerland.*

Competition from baseball was one concern; the other was that the Newark Velodrome, in 1926, was without its two greatest stars—Goullet and Kramer.

"Chapman's stalwarts were retiring and he was becoming increasingly dependent on foreign talent," Nye wrote in *Hearts of Lions*. "Rather than spend money to develop new young riders, he spent large sums to import

Freddie Spencer,
September 20, 1925,
the Newark Velodrome.
*Courtesy of Jeff Groman,
Jazz Sport LLC.*

experienced talent (from Australia and Europe), a propensity that was contributing to the sport's downfall in America."

Freddie Spencer of Plainfield was a young champion who did emerge in the mid-1920s. A headline in the September 14, 1925 edition of the *News*— "Freddie Spencer, Plainfield Youth, Is New Bicycle Sprint Champion"— heralded the New Jersey rider's achievement. Sixteen thousand fans turned out at the Newark saucer on September 20, 1925, to witness a ceremony where the twenty-three-year-old Spencer was lavished with a silver cup, flowers and gifts. Spencer was a dominant rider for the balance of the decade, clinching the national sprint crown in 1928 and 1929, and was runner-up in 1926 and 1927. In 1990, he was inducted into the U.S. Bicycling Hall of Fame.

Racing at the Newark Velodrome continued through the remainder of the 1920s. There was a serious fire at the track on July 11, 1926, which gutted the grandstands and roof. The blaze kindled memories of a similar incident at the old Vailsburg track twenty-two years earlier. Repairs were made, reportedly at a cost of $25,000, to finish the 1926 season.

View of fire damage at the Newark Velodrome, 1926. *Courtesy of Jeff Groman, Jazz Sport LLC.*

Cycling was losing its luster as fans, riders, promoters and journalists were painfully aware of the downward trend in attendance. Walter A. Bardgett, in his "On the Bell Lap" column in the July 1929 edition of *American Motorcyclist and Bicyclist* (*AM&B*), wrote that "the crowds at the Newark Velodrome this year have been poor and it may be after July 7 that the track will only race once a week and that on Wednesday nights."

Bardgett, writing in the September 1930 *AM&B*, said "the old cycle game is on stormy seas. Fire destroyed the New York Velodrome on Aug. 4 and by the time this (article) reaches cold type, the Providence Cycledrome (which opened on June 2, 1925) will be closed. The Newark track is in very bad condition and strips of tin have to be nailed over holes in the track at each race." An article in the October 30, 1929 edition of the *News* reported the 1928 and 1929 seasons were "disastrous as far as business is concerned."

The Newark Velodrome held its final races on Sunday, September 21, 1930. Two days later, a small, one-column article in the *News* announced the season had ended, and the track soon would be torn down. A separate article indicated the lease for the land on which the track sat was set to expire on January 1, 1931 and would not be renewed.

There was one footnote: the Alpine Wheelmen, a leading bicycle club in Newark, held its fourth annual two-hour team race at the Newark Velodrome on Sunday morning, September 28, 1930.

In the following months, there were occasional stories in the Newark newspapers about plans to revive the sport with a new velodrome, but it never came to pass.

The Avondale Saucer

In 1933, Joseph Miele, an entrepreneur from East Orange, stepped forward to fill the void left by the Newark Velodrome. His plan was to build a new velodrome in Nutley, a neighbor of Newark, confident he could rejuvenate the sport.

Miele made his fortune in the waste collection business and as a municipal contractor then branched out into the construction business. Columnist John Hall, writing in the April 19, 1933 edition of the *Elizabeth Daily Journal*, described Miele as a "contractor and sportsman" who loved bicycle racing.

Much like today, Nutley in the early 1930s was a civic-minded, suburban community with tree-lined streets. The April 14, 1933 edition of the *Nutley Sun* carried a page-one story that the town had issued a permit to build a bicycle track on a twelve-acre lot along the northern side of Park Avenue near River Road. The site was known as the Joyce Quarry, located in the town's Avondale section. Miele had purchased the property nine years earlier and used it to dispose of refuse from his business operations. The article stated Miele and his partners had established a franchise for racing with the National Cycling Association. On April 17, 1933, the Nutley Town Commission, led by Mayor Walter F. Reinheimer, unanimously granted Miele permission to build a cycling track.

However, the plan was controversial. James T. Brienza, a Newark attorney, presented a petition with 118 signatures to the commissioners that night, protesting the decision to build a velodrome. He was joined by a group of Nutley residents from the Avondale and Big Tree neighborhoods. Over one hundred "angry" cycling fans, strong supporters of Miele's velodrome proposal, turned out for the meeting to shout down the protestors.

"No one in the neighborhood liked the idea of building a cycling track," Frank A. Orechio, longtime publisher of the *Nutley Sun*, recalled during an interview in the early 1980s. Orechio was a politically active member of the predominantly Italian American community in the Big Tree and Avondale neighborhoods. He said residents resented the idea of being forced to live next to the noise, litter, crowds and traffic that a velodrome would bring. What was needed in Avondale at that time was a public park, he said.

"We've been trying for years to make Nutley a residential town," Mayor Reinheimer was quoted as saying at the April 17 meeting. "Perhaps we've tried too hard. I think we can stand a few more peanut bags scattered around. We certainly can stand more revenue in town. I think that the velodrome will be an asset to the community."

Cycling Comes to Nutley

Nutley Velodrome groundbreaking, April 19, 1933. Joseph Miele is pictured at the far left, wearing a hat and tie. Other dignitaries include cyclist Reggie McNamara (third from left, no hat) and Frank Kramer (third from right, with glasses and hat). *Courtesy of the Newark Public Library.*

Groundbreaking ceremonies for the velodrome were held April 19, 1933. Miele and his business associates, along with Mayor Reinheimer, Commissioners Young, Stager, Rife and DeMuro, police chief William J. Brown, and New Jersey governor A. Harry Moore, posed for newspaper photographers to promote the event.

Nutley resident Pat Mulvey, a nationally known figure in the construction of cycling tracks, supervised the operation, which had a workforce of thirty carpenters. The Sam Rachlin Co. supplied most of the construction materials. An estimated 400,000 feet of lumber would be used, with the track's riding surface made of cedar from Washington state. Grandstand seating for the velodrome was built to accommodate twelve thousand spectators. The track, at its highest point, stood as tall as a 3-story building. The July 16, 1933 edition of *Public Service News* reported that seventy-six one-thousand-watt lights were used to illuminate the track, grandstands and bleachers, main entrance and parking area, which could accommodate more than three thousand cars.

Miele hired Newark Velodrome legend Frank L. Kramer as an advisor and judge, hoping to capitalize on Kramer's prestige to help boost the fledgling operation. Kramer addressed the Nutley Rotary Club on May 18 to reassure the community that all activities at the saucer would maintain the highest level of integrity. Original plans called for a one-sixth-of-a-mile oval track—the size of most American cycling tracks of that era. However, Kramer persuaded Miele to build the track to one-seventh of a mile. Kramer reasoned that a smaller track design, with a steeper, banked riding surface and tighter turns, would generate more speed and fan excitement.

Harry Mendel joined Miele as director and manager of the Nutley Velodrome. Mendel worked in the management of the Newark Velodrome and the Woodbridge Speedway auto track and was a sports columnist for the *Newark Evening News*.

The cost of the project was estimated at $25,000. Construction began with Memorial Day set as the target date to open the track, but heavy spring rainstorms delayed work, and the first Sunday of June was chosen as the new date.

Practice run, motor-pace racers, Nutley Velodrome, 1933. *Courtesy of Jeff Groman, Jazz Sport LLC.*

Miele had signed the sport's top athletes to ensure the velodrome's opening day would be a world-class celebration. The field included Gerard Debaets of Belgium, Alfred Letourner of France, Franz Deulberg of Germany, Giovanni Manera of Italy, Charlie Jaeger of Newark and Paul Croley of Brooklyn. Other top riders signed to appear on opening day were Norman Hill, the speedster from San Jose, California, Australians Cecil Walker and Reggie McNamara, Newark's Tino Reboli and an amateur rider from Nutley named Martin Journey.

News photographers and one thousand fans gathered as Kramer rode the ceremonial first lap at the new velodrome on May 26, 1933, to christen the Nutley track. The *Nutley Sun*'s June 2, 1933 edition carried the headline "Bike World Luminaries Will Open New Velodrome Sunday Afternoon."

The Nutley Velodrome opened on Sunday, June 4, 1933, at 3:00 p.m. before a standing-room-only crowd. Miele's saucer was heralded as a worthy successor to the Newark Velodrome. Mayor Reinheimer fired the gun to start the featured twenty-five-mile Inaugural Stakes race, which was won by Brooklyn cyclist Croley. He received a silver loving cup from the mayor for his victory. The race was a motor-pace competition, which was touted as the premier event at the velodrome. Croley was paired with motorcycle rider Thomas Grimm of Maplewood. Second place went to the team of Debaets and Charles H. Stein of Brooklyn; third place, Deulberg and Willie Zipf of Hillside. Other featured races on opening day included Cecil Walker winning the pro one-mile match race. Hill won the pro three-mile, open-paced race, while Lloyd Thomas Jr. took the amateur one-mile novice match, which was the first event at the new saucer.

VICTOR HOPKINS

"Plow Boy" Victor Hopkins teamed with Jean Antenucci and won the featured twenty-five-mile motor-pace race on Wednesday, June 7, 1933—the first night race at the velodrome, which drew over seven thousand fans. Hopkins again took first place in the twenty-five-mile motor-pace on Sunday, June 11. One of the elite motor-pace racers of his era, Hopkins competed at the Nutley Velodrome during its first two seasons. Born to a single mother in Cedar Rapids, Iowa, on July 19, 1904, he was adopted by Mr. and Mrs. Jakob Hopkins, who died when he was nine, according to online information from the Iowa Soldier's Orphans' Home.

Hopkins won the American professional motor-pace title in 1926 and also raced in Europe. Veteran Iowa cyclist Worthington Longfellow Mitten, the

Vic Hopkins. *Courtesy of Jeff Groman, Jazz Sport LLC.*

founder of the Davenport Cycling Club, was a mentor for Hopkins. Nye, in a magazine article, wrote that Hopkins won a berth on the American Olympic cycling team and raced in the 1924 Paris Olympics. Hopkins competed in the 117-mile road race. He was riding the third-fastest time at the 30-mile mark of the competition but suffered a crash and a broken rear wheel when he hit a railroad-crossing gate. He changed the wheel but, unable to make up for the lost time, finished fifty-ninth in a field of seventy-two riders.

After the Olympics, Hopkins turned professional and was signed by John Chapman to compete in six-day races in Chicago and New York and motor-pace events in Newark. He suffered a broken collarbone in a training accident and was unable to defend his American motor-pace championship in 1927. The following year, he accepted an offer to compete in Europe and spent the next four years racing in France, Switzerland, Belgium and Germany. Miele enlisted him to compete at the Nutley Velodrome in 1933. Hopkins retired from professional cycling in 1934.

Harry Hopkins, Vic's son, and Nye told the story of how Vic Hopkins assisted fellow cyclist and friend Mathias Engel of Cologne, Germany. Hopkins met Engel in the early 1930s when the two were racing in Europe. Engel was a successful cyclist in Europe and also competed at the Nutley Velodrome. Engel returned to Cologne in the late 1930s and confronted the gathering terror of the Nazis. One night, in 1940, Engel and his family received a frantic phone call from a friend, informing them that the Gestapo was on its way to arrest his wife, who was Jewish. The Engel family barely escaped Germany and contacted Hopkins, at the time living in Nutley, who arranged for the transit of Engel and his family to the United States. As a result, Engel—forever grateful to Hopkins—settled in Nutley and opened a bike shop on Franklin Avenue.

Hopkins was inducted into the Nutley Hall of Fame in 2009, the Iowa Bicycle Racing Association Hall of Fame in 2005 and the U.S Bicycling Hall of Fame in 2006. He died in December 1969.

Pumping Pedals and Gas

Martin Journey, on opening day, took third place in the amateur "miss and out" race. Competing at the velodrome, the Nutley fans would be able to follow the progress of their hometown son. In a 1933 interview with Newark sports reporter Charley Travis, Journey paid tribute to his trainer, Benny Luscz. "My development this year is due to the great work of my trainer," Journey said, adding that Luscz had taught him the "finer points of the bike game." Luscz, in the same article, returned the praise, saying Journey was "the most conscientious" athlete on the Nutley circuit.

He was born in Nutley on October 18, 1913. His father, Michael Journey, was a professional cyclist who competed at the Newark Velodrome. Martin's career as a bike rider began in 1927 with races at Newark's Weequahic Park. As a fourteen-year-old, he finished 2nd in a field of 150 riders in a one-mile amateur race. Journey and partner John Seazholtz rode at the Newark Velodrome on September 28, 1930, and they won the Alpine Wheelmen's two-hour amateur team race. Under his dad's guidance, Journey joined two cycling clubs: first, the Alpine Wheelmen, and later, the Bay View Wheelmen. Journey took 2nd place in the Bay View Wheelmen's club championship races in 1930 and 1931. He hit his stride in 1932 when he won the twenty-five-mile cycle-path race at the Coney Island Velodrome.

A feature in the April 20, 1934 edition of the *Nutley Sun* profiled Journey's young career. "Last summer Nutley became the summer sphere on which the cycling industry rotated and Martin (Journey) found opportunity in his own backyard." The story described him as a frail youth who took a cue from his dad and turned to cycling as a way to strengthen his body. As an aspiring rider, Journey was learning the cycling trade from a diverse crew of savvy, international professionals at the Nutley saucer.

Martin Journey (bike rider on right, holding cup) at Weequahic Park, circa 1929. The bike rider at left is Freddy Graef. Willie Honeman (far right, wearing suit) is also pictured. *Courtesy of Jeff Groman, Jazz Sport LLC.*

The story said:

> *Weather permitting,* [Journey] *spins an hour each day on the track with Cecil Walker, who imparts valuable advice…On racing days he pays strict attention to his diet and partakes sparingly of chicken, potatoes, spinach and salad. Marty has the grit, stamina and determination and wants to turn professional next year. When not pumping pedals, he pumps gasoline at the family service station.*

Journey worked as an attendant at his dad's gas station, which was located in Nutley at the corner of Franklin Avenue and Harrison Street (today the site of a bakery). Journey's uncle, Joseph, also owned a gas station at the corner of Centre and Prospect Streets. It is still the site of a service station.

As a member of the Bay View Wheelmen, Journey won the national amateur all-around cycling championship during the second season at Nutley and was developing into a marketable, next-generation rider that the sport so desperately needed. A special reception was held in his honor on August 24, 1934, at the Nutley Bowling Club. Willie Coburn, a former six-day racer, organized the confab, and Journey was presented with a silver loving cup to celebrate his amateur-racing achievements.

Cycling Comes to Nutley

Michael Journey's Nutley gas station, corner of Franklin Avenue and Harrison Street, where his son, Martin Journey, worked. *Courtesy of the Nutley Historical Society.*

Martin Journey is paced by Eddie Root, who was a prominent bike rider at the Vailsburg and Newark velodromes. Root died on May 4, 1956, in East Orange, at the age of seventy-six. *Courtesy of Frank Cocchiola.*

Journey made his professional debut on June 5, 1935, winning the featured twenty-five-mile pro motor-pace race. His competition that day was Peden, Deulberg, Mike DeFilippo, Freddie Spencer, Jaeger and Victor Rausch. He continued on the pro circuit during the 1935 season, racing at velodromes in Cleveland, Chicago and Coney Island.

TORCHY, FRANCO AND TINO

The October 20, 1933 edition of the *Sun* recapped the successful first season at the Nutley Velodrome. The track had an overall attendance of 297,000 for thirty-five meets, with $60,000.00 paid out in prizes and salaries. Grandstand tickets were $0.75, while boxed and reserved seats were $1.00. A big event of the 1933 season was when twenty-eight-year-old George Dempsey of Sydney, Australia, on August 20, won the national five-mile pro championship. His competitors included Cecil Walker and Harris Horder, two other Australian riders, and Norman Hill.

The Nutley Velodrome's second season, which opened Sunday, April 1,

1934, was highlighted by news that veteran Canadian six-day champion William "Torchy" Peden and Italian star Franco Georgetti had signed to race. Ten thousand fans were on hand as Peden bested Ewald Wissel of Germany in the ten-mile motor-pace race. Former U.S. sprint champ Freddie Spencer defeated Australian George Dempsey in the four-mile pro handicap race, while Reboli teamed with Antenucci and won the twenty-five-mile motor-pace event.

Peden's debut at Nutley was just a quick stop on his

Autographed photo of Torchy Peden. *Courtesy of Jeff Groman, Jazz Sport LLC.*

busy schedule. According to newspaper reports, Peden had arrived by train at Newark's Penn Station that morning, having just won his twenty-first six-day race in Pittsburgh. After his appearance in Nutley, Peden got back on a train the next day and headed to Cleveland to ride in another six-day race.

Nutley fans had a great affection for Peden, who had a reputation as a hard-working, clean-living champion. A page-one story in the July 13, 1934 edition of the *Nutley Sun* offered a portrait of Peden as a "happy-go-lucky big fellow" who weighed in at 225 pounds and stood six feet, three inches tall. Peden touted his health-conscious lifestyle, saying the largest portion of his diet was made up of raw vegetables such as lettuce, carrots, turnips and cabbage. His favorite snack after a race was an egg sandwich.

Born in 1906, Peden grew up in Victoria, British Columbia, playing tennis and rugby. He also was a superior swimmer, and in 1926, he won the two-hundred-yard breaststroke title in the Canadian National Amateur championships. Two years later, Peden competed in the Canadian National Amateur bike races in Toronto and qualified for the Canadian Olympic cycling team. He noted in the article that, during his long and successful career as a bike racer, the 1928 Olympics, held in Amsterdam, the Netherlands, was his biggest thrill.

After the Olympics, he remained in Europe and competed in races held in Warsaw, London, Paris and Berlin. Following his tour of Europe, Peden returned to Canada and rode in his first six-day bike race in October 1929 at the Forum in Montreal. His nickname "Torchy" was bestowed on him by Canadian sports journalists. He recalled how one writer described him as "Big Bill Peden with his torch-colored hair blowing in the wind." Torchy died in Chicago on January 25, 1980, at the age of seventy-three, according to the online Six-Day Racing bio by Arnold Devlin. Torchy is a member of the Canadian Sports Hall of Fame.

Franco Georgetti made his Nutley debut on April 29, winning the twenty-five-mile motor-pace race, paced by Zipf. Three days before the race, Georgetti had arrived in New York on the Italian ocean liner *Rex*. News articles in 1934 described him as the "highest-paid cycling star in the world." An article in *Time* magazine estimated Georgetti's annual earnings at $28,000. The story also portrayed him as a "small, knocked-kneed" Italian who maintained a ritual of having a barber shave him on the morning of every race.

When he arrived in Nutley at the age of thirty-one, Georgetti jousted with reporters, boasting that he wasn't past his prime and that he was "as good as ever." Born October 13, 1902, in Varese, Italy, Georgetti (some sources

BICYCLE AND MOTOR-PACED RACES

Nutley *Velodrome*

Meet No. 4
Sunday, April 22
1934

Official
Programme

10¢

FRANCO GEORGETTI
Motor Paced Champion of America, 1927-1933
Courtesy of Newark Star-Eagle

Nutley Velodrome program, April 22, 1934, featuring cover photo of Franco Georgetti. *Courtesy of Jeff Groman, Jazz Sport LLC.*

spell his name Giorgetti) took an interest in cycling as a teenager. He came from a prominent family in Milan and was groomed to go into the printing and bookbinding business. He won a gold medal in the 1920 Summer Olympics held in Antwerp, Belgium, as part of a men's team pursuit competition. He was the winner of eleven six-day races and captured four American motor-pace championships (1927–1930). He died March 18, 1983, in Bovisio Masciago, Monza e Brianza, Italy.

Tino Reboli, interviewed at his Nutley home in the early 1980s, proudly described his "badge of honor" from his racing days: his right knee, which had been replaced with an artificial joint. "The doctor said it looked like a mouse had been inside my knee for years, gnawing away at it," he said, with a smile. In his prime, Reboli would ride seventy-five miles a day and occasionally trained alongside heavyweight boxing contender Tony Galento in the South Orange Mountains.

Growing up on Bank Street in Newark, Reboli's neighbors encouraged him to take up cycling. A *Newark Sunday Call* article by Charley Travis said Reboli captured the Newark and national junior road race championships in 1929. He won the state senior road race titles in 1931 and 1932. After capturing his second New Jersey road racing title in 1932, Reboli took part in a competition sanctioned by the NCA to select candidates for the Olympic team that year. Weequahic Park in Newark was the site of qualifying races. With the local fans cheering him on, Reboli came away with victories in the one-mile and three-mile races for senior amateurs. Unfortunately, the NCA was unable to raise sufficient money to sponsor him for the trip to Los Angeles Summer Olympics.

Reboli's most prized keepsake from his racing days was the bike designed and built for him by John "Pop" Brennan. "All the riders from the velodrome went to Pop for bikes," he said. To maintain a competitive edge, top cyclists invested in custom-made bicycles. Pop Brennan was the most sought-after bicycle craftsman in New Jersey during the golden era. Cycling old-timers lauded Brennan and his sons, Bill and Jackie, as the best bicycle mechanics.

Tino Reboli at the Nutley Velodrome. *Courtesy of Jeff Groman, Jazz Sport LLC.*

Pop Brennan was inducted in 1996 into the U.S. Bicycling Hall of Fame, Davis, California. According to information on the website of the California Bicycle Museum, Brennan gained his insights and skill in metalworking during his first career as a chandelier maker. He transferred his skills in steel tube bending and joining for the production of bicycle frames and handlebars, seizing business opportunities to satisfy the demanding athletes who competed at the Newark and Nutley Velodromes.

Professional cycling carried Reboli to competitions in Chicago, Cleveland and Buffalo and six-day races at Madison Square Garden. Chester A. Tino Reboli Jr. retired from racing in 1946 and died on November 18, 1985, at the age of seventy-two.

Like bike riders, motor-pace motorcycle drivers at the Nutley track had their own fan following. Clad in leather riding outfits, the motorcycle men thrived on their daredevil image. Jean Antenucci was the most popular motorcycle pacer at the Nutley Velodrome. He worked out of a Nutley

Motor-pace motorcycle riders at the Nutley Velodrome in April 1935. Pictured (from left) are Orlando Piani, Otto Miller, Mike Santarpia (who promoted races at the track in 1940), Eddie Root, Willie Marino and Gordon Walker. *Courtesy of the Newark Public Library.*

garage—G&A Auto Wreckers—owned by Al and Ken Gorman. According to a 1972 Associated Press article, Antenucci, who went by the nickname Gigi, was born in 1900 in Furci, Italy. He came to America with his parents at age three and grew up in Rhode Island.

"I used to hang around the Providence Velodrome and watched some of the great motor-pacers and bike riders," he told sports columnist Augie Lio in an interview published March 13, 1973, in the *Herald-News*. "You might say I got the itch. So I bought my own motorcycle and hung around waiting for a break."

His break came when he was part of a winning motor-pace team at a race in Philadelphia in 1919. He competed as a motor-pace motorcyclist in Europe and Australia during the 1920s and eventually landed in Nutley to take advantage of racing opportunities at the new saucer. Gigi died on April 12, 1975.

Another leading motor-pace man at the Nutley track was Charles Henry Stein. Stein was an American amateur cycling sprint champion in 1908.

Motor-pace motorcycle riders at the Nutley Velodrome on September 30, 1933. Pictured (from left) are Charles Stein, Tom Grimm, Jimmy Ferruolo, William Zipf, Jean Antenucci and Frank Jeehan. *Courtesy of the Newark Public Library.*

He turned pro later that year and competed at tracks throughout North America. Born on October 9, 1886, in Brooklyn, New York, Stein moved his family to Nutley in 1933. He died on April 29, 1957.

STARS AND STRIPES

Famed American sprinter and Newark native Bill Honeman made his first appearance at the Nutley track on June 14, 1933, winning the one-mile pro race. Honeman and his eye-catching racing outfit made a patriotic fashion statement when he landed at the Nutley saucer, following a two-year stint of racing in Europe.

An article by Nye said the fashion-conscious French wanted Honeman to compete in a more colorful racing garb to better identify him as the U.S. national champion. The United States—unlike European countries that dressed their national champions in jerseys made of silk, using the colors of

Willie Honeman, Norman Hill and Franco Georgetti (left to right) pose at the Nutley Velodrome, 1934. Honeman is wearing his famous stars and stripes jersey. *Courtesy of Jeff Groman, Jazz Sport LLC.*

their respective national flags—didn't have such recognizable outfits for its cyclists. As a result, a Paris sports shop designed the classic stars and stripes jersey for Honeman.

When Honeman arrived at the Nutley Velodrome, he brought with him the stars and stripes jersey, which became a local and then national sensation. Nye said the red, white and blue outfit promptly caught on as the official national champion's jersey. Both of the American national governing bodies for the sport of cycling—the National Cycling Association (for professionals) and the Amateur Bicycle League of America—officially adopted the stars and stripes jersey.

Honeman became the U.S. junior national road and track champion at sixteen in 1924. He turned pro in 1928 and finished second (to Freddie Spencer) in the American sprint championship in 1929. He did win the quarter-mile national championship on June 4, 1930 in Newark. Honeman traveled to Europe in the summer of 1930, racing in Brussels and the Velodrome d'Hiver in Paris, an indoor track that could accommodate up to fifteen thousand spectators and was famous for its giant skylight.

As the 1934 season drew to a close, Honeman was honored as the sprint champion of America. He received a floral crown from Kramer on Sunday, September 30, and was showered with gifts at the Nutley saucer. Later that night, he was the guest of honor at a banquet hosted by the Bay View

Willie Honeman. *Courtesy of Jeff Groman, Jazz Sport LLC.*

Wheelmen. He also won the American national pro championship at the Nutley Velodrome in 1935 and 1936 and left the legacy of his jersey to designate U.S. champions.

After retiring, Honeman remained active in the sport. He moved to California and became involved with the Encino Velodrome. He was inducted into the U.S. Bicycling Hall of Fame in 1994 and died two years later, on August 19—one day before his eighty-eighth birthday.

THE ODD COUPLE

Two accomplished European cyclists—Alfred Letourner, a Frenchman, and Gerard Debaets, a Belgian—were the guests of honor at a dinner in New York City on March 5, 1933, which was hosted by Unione Sportiva Italiana, a sports club founded in 1908. The duo had just won the fifty-fourth international six-day race at Madison Square Garden, and they soon would become fixtures at the Nutley track.

Alfred Letourner (left) and Gerard Debaets, undated, following a six-day race victory. *Courtesy of Jeff Groman, Jazz Sport LLC.*

Letourner and Debaets, during the 1932–1933 winter indoor cycling season, won four consecutive six-day race competitions in New York, Chicago, Montreal and Toronto. Though they were a successful team on the six-day circuit, Debaets and Letourner were bitter rivals at the Nutley saucer. In one episode, following a motor-pace race on August 28, 1933, Letourner had a heated confrontation with Debaets and referee Kramer. Letourner was penalized for an alleged foul, but he vigorously complained to Kramer that Debaets actually was the guilty party.

John Kieran, in his "Sports of the Times" column published on March 3, 1935, picked up on this volatile element in their friendship. "Debaets, he ees variy funny," Kieran wrote, quoting the "snappy" Letourner phonetically in the article to capture his distinctive French accent. "When we are the team, we are the great friends. But when we are not the team—ooh la la! We are the great enemies. But he ees a fine partner."

Debaets, interviewed by Kieran later that year, described the colorful relationship from his own perspective. "I do not say he (Letourner) is the best partner, but he is the smartest; oh, very much," Debaets was quoted in a November 29, 1935 column. "And he has what you call the courage. Maybe he is the best partner, but I do not tell him so. I tell him I am the best partner and he is lucky (to have me)."

During the interview, while he boasted of his many injuries from cycling— dislocated shoulders, broken ribs, cuts and scrapes—Debaets also revealed far more serious physical traumas, such as being shot in the legs and ankle by German soldiers who occupied his country during World War I. He told

Norman Hill (left) and Gerard Debaets toss a medicine ball during a late winter/early spring workout session. *Courtesy of Jeff Groman, Jazz Sport LLC.*

Kieran harrowing stories of being beaten, thrown into prison and having a revolver held to his head when he once was accused of being a spy.

After the war, when he became a cyclist, he told the tale of traveling to Munich by train to compete in a race:

> *When the train stopped at a station, I look on the platform and yell: "Karl, Karl." It is this old (German) fellow who guarded me in the War. He looks, he looks—ah! He knows me. I must get off the train and go to his house. We have a fine time and he laughs when I tell him I was right about the Germans leaving my country.*

Debaets, by his count, won eighteen six-day races (eight with Letourner). He placed first in the 1925 Belgian National Road Racing Championship, the 1925 Paris-Bruxelles race and the Tour of Flanders race in 1924 and 1927. He was born on April 17, 1899, in Courtrai, Belgium. Following his retirement in 1945, he opened a bicycle shop in Paterson and resided in Fair Lawn and North Haledon. He died of a heart attack on April 27, 1959.

Gerard Debaets. *Courtesy of Jeff Groman, Jazz Sport LLC.*

Letourner earned a reputation as a controversial rider at the Nutley saucer, according to newspaper articles of the day and later confirmed by the veteran cyclists who knew him. He won the American motor-pace championship for the third consecutive year on the final day of the second season—September 26, 1934.

Known for his fiery temper, the Frenchman sometimes was booed by the Nutley fans for what the press described as his "prima donna antics." A page-one article in the August 31, 1934 edition of the *Nutley Sun* mentioned an incident where Letourner "found himself at odds with police in a River Road tavern last Wednesday night."

His brash style may have been a reflection of his turbulent life while growing up in France. He was born July 25, 1907, in Amiens, a town located seventy-five miles north of Paris. His father, a blacksmith, taught young Alf to ride a bicycle at an early age. His parents had a stormy relationship and separated, which resulted in young Alf being sent to live with an uncle, who worked on a dairy farm. Letourner's father served in the French army during World War I. He was captured by the Germans in 1917 and was executed, along with fourteen other prisoners.

When the war ended, Letourner's mother remarried, but according to a page-one article in the September 28, 1934 edition of the *Sun*, Letourner's stepfather drove him away. The feature, written by Chester Bellows, described Letourner as a "homeless waif" at the age of thirteen. Young Alf drifted to Paris and worked as a delivery boy, carrying packages on a three-wheel bicycle and running errands for various merchants. Letourner estimated that he rode his bike nearly sixty miles a day on his delivery route.

In 1923, Letourner met Edmond Jacquelin, a French sports hero and the 1900 world sprint cycling champion. With Jacquelin as his mentor, Letourner began to train as a cyclist. However, the two soon hit hard times. Jacquelin was a man who spent his money fast, and they became destitute. In a desperate move, Jacquelin hocked a "magnificent" stopwatch that was presented to him in 1900 by "popular subscription" of the people of France to honor his cycling achievements. According to Letourner, this timepiece was Jacquelin's prized possession.

When the French cycling community learned of Jacquelin's financial difficulties, they staged a benefit for him. The effort raised cash that Jacquelin used to purchase a dirt cycling track in Neuilly-sur-Seine, a western suburb of Paris. Letourner and Jacquelin still were strapped financially and were forced to sleep on the floor of an old garage on the track property.

Guided by Jacquelin, Letourner began to win amateur races. He suffered a serious injury to his right leg, but after it healed, Letourner turned professional in 1927 and resumed his cycling career, putting together a string of victories throughout Europe. That success propelled him to the North American circuit.

While he lived to see his disciple's early success in cycling, Jacquelin died in 1931. But the article by Bellows, in addition to citing the Frenchman's racing accomplishments, offered a glimpse into Letourner's hidden sentimental nature—a contrast to his abrasive reputation. Following Jacquelin's death, Letourner returned to France. His mission was to reclaim his mentor's treasured stopwatch. Bellows wrote the Frenchman kept the watch with him always. Letourner said the watch inspired him and kept him grounded—a private reminder of the days "when life was a pretty tough proposition." He died on January 4, 1975, in New York City.

"TRACK TRIBULATIONS"

The Nutley Velodrome's first two seasons—1933 and 1934—proved successful, as the saucer filled the vacuum left by the Newark Velodrome. Bike races drew an average gate of more than eight thousand fans. Nutley was a magnet for top international cyclists, and the town's dateline was flashed throughout the world, as wire services picked up the cycling news posted by New Jersey newspapers.

Marty Pedersen, a 1935 graduate of West Orange High School, recalled driving to Nutley with his pal Joe Wannemacher to catch the Wednesday night races. Interviewed in 2008, Pedersen, who became a musician, said his most vivid memory of the velodrome was Joe Basile and His Popular Band, which performed in the track's infield. He said that when the riders entered the bell lap, Basile's ensemble would play rousing music to energize the crowd and amplify the drama at the finish line. He also remembered the "blue cloud" that hung over the saucer during evening races, as the bright stadium lamps illuminated the thick fog of cigarette smoke rising from the grandstands.

"The riders were such wonderful athletes," Pedersen said, noting that the festive atmosphere of the Wednesday night races offered a much-needed diversion from the humdrum days of Depression-era life. "Those were tough, difficult times. The bike races at the velodrome were exciting. People went there to get a break and enjoy themselves."

Miele said business was so good during the first two seasons that the track generated enough revenue to pay for construction and operating expenses

Nutley's Bell Lap Tavern, circa 1950, located at the corner of Washington and Park Avenues, was named for the "bell lap," or final lap of a race. It was a favorite watering hole for the velodrome crowd. *Courtesy of Mary O'Neill.*

Cycling Comes to Nutley

Norman Hill (top) and Franco Georgetti race at the Nutley Velodrome. *Courtesy of Jeff Groman, Jazz Sport LLC.*

after two seasons, rather than the five to seven he originally had projected. "When I built the velodrome, I didn't expect to get rich from it," Miele was quoted as saying in 1933, shortly after the saucer opened. "I just wanted to give bike fans a break and help to promote the sport."

But there was trouble brewing at the saucer. The partnership of Miele and Mendel fractured in January 1935, as Mendel abruptly announced he was leaving Nutley to manage the rival Coney Island Velodrome, which opened July 19, 1930.

Frank Sempsa, a former chairman of the board of controls for the National Cycling Association, recalled during an interview in the early 1980s that Mendel quietly had gone to Europe at the end of the 1934 season to enlist riders for 1935. He said a dispute erupted between Miele and Mendel over money, percentage of profits and the signing of riders. "When they (Miele and Mendel) split up, that was the beginning of the end. Things were never the same."

Willie Ratner, in a February 6, 1942 column, recalling the dispute, wrote that Mendel—fearful Miele would not renew his contract as manager at the Nutley saucer—jumped to the Coney Island track. Mendel signed most of the prominent riders to come with him, "feeling their absence at Nutley would break that track," according to Ratner. "It did, to a certain extent, but Mendel's venture at Coney Island was a failure." Letourner, Georgetti, Reboli, Debaets, Honeman, Wissel and Hill aligned themselves with Mendel at Coney Island. Miele, quoted in the *Sun* on March 22, 1935, was diplomatic, saying he was agreeable to riders competing at both tracks.

Aside from the nuances of their disagreement, the clash between Miele and Mendel deflated what was left of the professional cycling circuit. The 1935 season opened April 14 on a chilly Sunday afternoon, with five thousand fans on hand. Nutley resident Ray Blum—who later represented the United States as a speed skater at 1948 Winter Olympics in St. Moritz, Switzerland—made his first appearance at the velodrome and won the one-mile novice event. Journey placed second in a separate amateur handicap race, and the following month, he announced his decision to join the professional ranks.

Nutley Sun sports columnist Bill Clay, in a May 17, 1935 column titled "Track Tribulations," took stock

Nutley Velodrome program, June 9, 1935, featuring a cover photo of Australian rider Cecil Walker. *Courtesy of Jeff Groman, Jazz Sport LLC.*

of the Nutley/Coney Island controversy. "While this dog-eat-dog business between Miele and Mendel rages, the fans attracted to both velodromes are handed the worst of it," he wrote. Clay grumbled that the riders who remained in Nutley were "second-rate" and warned that, if the "condition isn't remedied, many of the forty-centers (paying fans) will be spending their spare time at the ballparks."

Arthur J. Lea Mond, a member of Miele's management team, responded to Clay's commentary one week later with a letter published in the *Sun*'s May 24 edition.

> *Is Mr. Clay qualified to put a yardstick on the riders at both tracks? Mr. Clay is either biased or doesn't know what he is talking about. It has been the purpose of the owner, Joseph Miele, from the very moment he started construction of the Nutley track to conduct the velodrome…on a clean, honest, dignified plane. We have a very heavy investment in the track and we have secured, through our races, consistent and good publicity throughout the world.*

Midway through the season, Miele and Mendel made peace, with Kramer serving as the intermediary. The June 21, 1935 edition of the *Sun* reported the "war" between Miele and Mendel "ended in a draw." Two weeks later, in the July 5 edition, the headline on the lead story read: "Pace Chasers All Back as Coney Island Closes." The *Sun* reported riders were returning to Nutley, as the Coney Island track was forced to "temporarily" shut down. Coney Island occasionally hosted races throughout the late 1930s, as well as in August and September 1941. In the mid-1950s, the structure was razed to make way for the Luna Park Mitchell Lama Housing project, according to Brooklyn cycling historian Harry Schwartzman.

"So ends the 1935 bike war," the *Sun*'s June 21 story declared. "Why any rider would attempt to buck Joe Miele, the man who for two years has contributed so much of his time and energy to a lone fight to bring bike racing back as a popular sport, is a bit of an enigma."

Despite the truce between Miele and Mendel, there were telltale signs the Nutley track still was having difficulties. Attendance during the 1935 season was down considerably, compared with 1933 and 1934, according to press reports. The *Sun* sports column "Bike Track Oddments" noted the velodrome was showing wear and tear from three seasons of pounding. The same column, on September 6, 1935, penned by Walt Maloney, reflected the discontent he saw among fans. "One thing is for certain," Maloney

Five-mile race on April 14, 1935, at the Nutley Velodrome, showing the track's sharply banked curve. *Courtesy of the Newark Public Library.*

wrote, "Joe Miele will have to revamp the motor-pace circus so that the fans stop yawning."

Carpenters and painters were busy with maintenance at the Nutley saucer during the early spring of 1936, looking to dress up "America's outdoor cycling center," as proclaimed in a page-one story in the April 3, 1936 edition of the *Nutley Sun*. However, some sports writers complained the track was in a state of disrepair—an outward sign of the bike game's growing difficulties. Maloney quipped that "if they keep patching the track, it'll be all tin by the end of the season."

The 1936 season opened on April 19, with Journey defeating Letourner, Georgetti, DeFilippo and Walthour in the featured twenty-five-mile motor-pace race before a crowd of three thousand. Attendance remained tepid that season, and on July 16, 1936, Miele announced he was leaving the cycling game. "Business matters have developed, making it impossible for me to continue to promote bike racing," he told reporters.

Miele leased the velodrome's operations to cycling legend Alf Goullet and Edward J. Malone. The *Sun*'s lead story on July 17, 1936, reported the deal

Nutley Velodrome, infield judge's and announcer's stand, on June 6, 1934. *Courtesy of the Newark Public Library.*

Five-mile race at the Nutley Velodrome in May 1936. *Courtesy of the Newark Public Library.*

Norman Hill wins the five-mile race on April 19, 1936, at the Nutley Velodrome. The figure on the far right with dark coat and derby is Frank Kramer. *Courtesy of the Newark Public Library.*

was a three-year agreement. "The change of control came as a surprise to the public, but there have been rumors for several months that Miele and his associates wanted to get out of the bike game," the article said.

Goullet was quoted as being optimistic that he and his partner could "bring the cycling game back." He felt there was too much emphasis on motor-pace racing. "Variety is what we need and new talent must be developed," he declared.

"The riders came to me about running the velodrome," Goullet said in an interview more than forty years later, recalling that Australian cyclist Cecil Walker served as spokesman for the athletes.

However, attendance remained lackluster despite the change in management. Ratner, in his September 22, 1936 column, reported that a confrontation had taken place at the Nutley saucer between riders and management. Ratner said cyclists and motor-pace men demanded that all prize money be placed in the hands of respected velodrome referee Kramer before the start of races to guarantee that winners would be paid. Kramer took the demands to Goullet and Malone, who said that, due to low box office receipts, they would have to provide the riders with checks rather than cash. The riders declined this arrangement and walked out, refusing to compete at the track.

"The walkout was the culmination of a long series of disagreements between management and pro and amateur riders," Ratner wrote. "The riders are not to be blamed for the fiasco. They had every reason to ask for protection."

Goullet and Malone made another attempt to hold races in 1937, but by August 5, the track was forced to close due to poor attendance.

GRAVE 2277

One night in mid-September 1937, Martin Journey went to visit his younger cousin, Walt Journey, who was a patient at SoHo Hospital in Belleville. It would be the last time Walt would see his favorite cousin. Walt, age eleven, was suffering from lead poisoning.

"Marty was leaving for Australia the next day," Walt Journey recalled during an interview in 2005. "I was sick, but I wanted to wish him good luck. He wanted to see me before he left. He was concerned about me and wanted to say goodbye."

During the winter of 1936–1937, Martin Journey had traveled to Buenos Aires, Argentina, to compete on the South American racing circuit, riding under Goullet's leadership. The day after his visit with Walt at the hospital, Martin Journey traveled to Vancouver, Canada, boarded an ocean liner and headed for Australia to continue his promising racing career.

Martin Journey died unexpectedly in Melbourne on November 26, 1937. The cause of his death was a heart disorder. News accounts said that, eight days before his death, Journey had been admitted to a health clinic and was under the care of a heart specialist. Cecil Walker was the first to receive word of Journey's passing and broke the news to Journey's family. Walker had encouraged Journey to travel to Australia to test his talents against top international bike riders.

A photocopy of a tattered Australian newspaper clipping provided by Walt Journey included a two-column picture of Martin Journey's flag-draped casket being carried down the steps of Melbourne's Saint Patrick's Cathedral. The article said Father R. Tarten of the Fathers of the Blessed Sacrament celebrated the requiem Mass on December 1, 1937.

Pallbearers included W. Maddock, president of the Australian Federal Cycling Union, and C. Perugia, president of the Victorian Amateur Cycling Union.

Sorrow for the hometown cycling son was palpable as the *Nutley Sun*, in its December 3, 1937 edition, carried a page one headline that said: "Journey Buried in Australia." The story, which said the young rider had died from an "athletic heart," indicated an epidemic of infantile paralysis prevented Journey's body from being returned to the New Jersey community. A column by Walt Maloney in the same edition offered a eulogy, recalling Journey's sportsmanship as well as his athletic talents. "Unfortunately, (Journey) rose in the sport when it was at its lowest ebb. He will be a champion where he has gone."

Journey is buried at Fawkner Crematorium and Memorial Park, Fawkner, Victoria, Australia, Roman Catholic Compartment 0, Grave 2277.

Martin Journey's grave site. *Courtesy of Fawkner Crematorium and Memorial Park, Fawkner, Victoria, Australia.*

Midget Cars

With bicycle races foundering, the December 17, 1937 *Nutley Sun* carried a front-page story that said town commissioners had granted Jack Kochman of Eastern Speedway Inc. a license to run "midget" auto races at the wooden saucer. The car races, the article said, would help to put the velodrome back on "the black side of the financial ledger," offsetting the decline of the cycling game. Miele went before commissioners and asked them to approve the request, saying he would install a new pine-board track surface and safety features for the 1938 season. Many were concerned about the dangers of racing cars on a wooden saucer designed for bicycles. Midget cars, with their powerful engines, typically reached speeds of more than seventy-five miles per hour and featured an open-cockpit chassis.

After structural improvements were made to accommodate the cars and metal fencing and guardrails were installed to shield spectators, midget auto racing made its debut at the Nutley Velodrome on April 3, 1938. More than eight thousand fans filled the grandstands. There were two accidents

Midget car races, Nutley Velodrome, 1938. *Courtesy of the Newark Public Library.*

on opening day. First, Vern Orenduff, a twenty-nine-year-old Floridian, narrowly escaped serious injury when his car crashed and overturned; then, Ken Fowler of Dayton, Ohio, suffered a mishap, as his car nearly vaulted into the stands, injuring fourteen spectators. Fowler fractured his arm, while his car was left dangling atop the guardrail.

The opening-day incidents foreshadowed three fatal accidents: Charlie Helliker, on October 9, 1938; Henry Guerand on April 2, 1939 (the infamous decapitation tragedy); and Karl Hattel on August 26, 1939. Following Hattel's death, Essex County prosecutors put a halt to the midget races. Nutley commissioners, on September 8, 1939, announced that a town referendum would be held to let residents decide the fate of midget car races. The ballot question, drawn up by Commissioner Rife, asked: "Shall the Board of Commissioners of Nutley grant a permit for operation of midget auto races at the velodrome?" Nutley voters struck down midget auto racing on November 10, 1939, by a vote of 2,161 to 770.

As the midget car drama unfolded, there was an ill-fated attempt to bring cycling back to the velodrome. Commissioners approved a request to hold bike races on Sunday night, July 30, 1939. Carmine Bilotti, a former associate of Harry Mendel, headed a group known as the Nutley Cycling Association, which would organize the races. An article in the August 11, 1939 edition of the *Sun* said bike riders, "who did their best to convince a small but enthusiastic crowd," remained hopeful attendance would increase.

Bilotti said he wanted to rebuild the fan base for cycling "to where riders and everyone else could make a living." Bike races were staged in August and September 1939, but the grandstands remained empty. An article in the September 29, 1939 *Sun* said "Bilotti attempted a comeback with 'pedal pushers' but could not draw enough customers to pay for the electric lights."

FOR WHOM THE BELL (LAP) TOLLS

There was a final attempt to hold cycling at the velodrome. A page-one article in the July 12, 1940 edition of the *Sun* carried the headline "Cycling Tries Comeback at Velodrome Tonight." Commissioners on June 25 approved a proposal by sports promoter Mike Santarpia, who had organized bike races at the rival Coney Island track, and Torchy Peden. The *Sun* described the effort as "a case of do or die" for bike racing at the velodrome. Miele was prepared to close and demolish the track if the Santarpia-Peden effort proved unsuccessful.

Cycling Comes to Nutley

The featured event for opening night was a twenty-five-mile motor-pace race that included Reboli, Letourner, Debaets and DeFilippo. Two pro cyclists from Germany—Gustave Kilian and Heinz Vopel—were the headliners in a twenty-mile pro race. In addition, Nutley resident Blum was on the card, touted as "one of the best bets in the amateur field."

Mickey Franciose, a Montclair resident and a former amateur titleholder, arrived in Nutley after a year of competing in Australia. Other riders that summer included Ewald Wissel, Danny Esposito, Jimmy Walthour, Angelo DeBacco and George Shipman. Races were held throughout July and August, but fan turnout was disappointing. Franciose won the four-mile event on September 6, while Kilian captured the twenty-five-mile motor-pace race.

Nutley Velodrome, July 1940. *Courtesy of the Newark Public Library.*

September 15, 1940, a Sunday afternoon, marked the final day of races at the Nutley Velodrome. The saucer closed its gates for the last time. The golden era of U.S. velodrome cycling had come to an end.

The saucer sat idle for eighteen months. Ratner, in his February 6, 1942 column, announced that the Nutley track was being torn down. "A demolition permit has been obtained from the building department of the town of Nutley and, board by board, the structure is being carted away," Ratner wrote. "The once-famous track...soon will be no more."

The column applauded Miele's effort to build the saucer in an attempt to boost the sport of professional cycling. "Miele, whose hobby was bicycle racing, once was a trainer and handler of Pete Drobach, one of the prominent professionals in the early days of the (Newark) Velodrome. Little did Miele think that some day he would build a track to revive the sport he loved so much." Ratner, born in Newark in 1895, covered sports for the *News* for five decades and died on April 3, 1980.

Nutley eventually acquired the property where the velodrome had stood, along with adjacent tracts of land. Town voters eventually approved a $30,000 bond issue to develop a park and public playground at the site.

Joseph Miele died on February 20, 1973, at Saint Mary's Hospital, Orange, at the age of eighty-one. An obituary in the February 21, 1973 edition of the *Star-Ledger* noted that Miele, an army air corps veteran during World War I, was a successful businessman who, in addition to his New Jersey operations, had interests in gold mines in South America.

The Nutley Velodrome was all but forgotten in the decades that followed, but the town recaptured some of its cycling heritage in May 1972 with the Tour of Nutley criterium. Championed by Nutley commissioner Frank A. Cocchiola, along with Peloton Sports Inc. and the Nutley Bicycle Club, the race drew top international bicycle riders to the town.

The Tour of Nutley commemorated the fiftieth anniversary of the opening of the Nutley Velodrome on May 29, 1983. Golden-era riders were special guests at various ceremonies that day, including a nostalgic reunion breakfast held at the Nutley Elks lodge on Chestnut Street.

Twenty-five years later, the Nutley Museum held a diamond-anniversary celebration of the Nutley Velodrome on June 4, 2008, sponsored by the Nutley Historical Society. The township, led by Mayor Joanne Cocchiola (Frank's daughter), paid tribute to the seventy-fifth anniversary of the velodrome through an official proclamation. "Whereas, the mayor and board of commissioners of Nutley would like to honor the Nutley Velodrome as a symbol of Nutley's history, be it proclaimed that June 4, 2008 is Nutley Velodrome Day."

Chapter 5

THE TOUR OF SOMERVILLE

COMMUTING TO BOUND BROOK

A bike rider from Somerville won the pro two-mile handicap race at the Nutley Velodrome on Wednesday, July 26, 1933. His name was Frederick William Kugler. In years to come, people would know him as "Pop."

Kugler created the Tour of Somerville, the world-famous criterium and New Jersey's renowned "Kentucky Derby of Cycling." Driven by his fascination with bicycle riding and dedication to community service, Pop Kugler's tour would chart a new course for cycling history in the Garden State.

Born in Somerville on June 4, 1900, Pop Kugler's love for cycling was a family affair, according to his daughter, Mildred. Interviewed in March 2010, she said her grandfather, Fred Kugler Sr., a high-wheel racer, inspired her father. Pop's dad founded the Somerset Wheelmen in 1912. In addition to cycling, both father and son served Somerville as volunteer firemen.

In an article written by Pop in the May 23, 1987 special section on the Tour of Somerville published by the *Courier-News*, he revealed that he became a bike rider out of financial necessity. In 1916, he was hired by American Engine Works in Bound Brook, located six miles from his Somerville home. The cost of a trolley ride was a nickel each way—a significant chunk of his six-day-a-week salary of $2.20. Compelled by the economics of the situation, he began riding his bike to work.

"After two years of riding a bike 12 miles a day, six days a week, I entered a few races and in 1918 started riding the velodromes of Newark, Philadelphia and New York," he wrote.

Fortified by his machinist skills, Pop eventually began working in his father's bicycle shop. He took over the business and, in 1925, moved the shop to 11½ Davenport Street in downtown Somerville. Two years later, as a prelude to the Tour of Somerville, Kugler organized the Somerville 25-Mile Classic, which was held May 30, 1927.

A feature article in a 1936 edition of the *Somerset Messenger* traced Pop's career highlights as a cyclist. In June 1926, he placed second in a one-hundred-mile, New York to Philadelphia amateur road race. Two years later, he finished third in the state's national Olympic tryouts and placed fifth overall in the New Jersey all-around championship. He turned pro in 1928 and won the 1936 U.S. National Tandem championship, teaming with Russell Allen.

"Pop lived at a time when the sport was going through a period of transition. He knew it was the end of an era; that professional track racing had died," said Joe Saling, a former bike racer who has served as the tour's announcer since the early 1960s.

Tour of Somerville. *Courtesy of Middle Earth, Bridgewater, Tour of Somerville Archives.*

In 1940, there only were a limited number of national U.S. amateur cycling championship competitions for senior men, senior women and juniors. The Amateur Bicycle League of America sanctioned national races. By the mid-1940s, cycling in America had gone "underground," with only one thousand active U.S. amateur riders, according Jack Simes III, a member of the U.S. Bicycling Hall of Fame and a two-time winner of the tour.

"There was no structure to the sport in America," Simes said. "The pro circuit had collapsed and the stars of the velodrome era had long since retired. It was the regional cycling clubs that kept the sport alive."

MILDRED, HARRY AND FURMAN

Somerville resident Ron Czajkowski, who attended his first tour in 1957 at the age of eight and for thirty years has served as the event's self-described "armchair historian," said Pop Kugler continued the family tradition by passing on his love of cycling to his son and three daughters: Furman, Mildred, Shirley and Anna. By the late 1930s, Pop had retired from racing and focused on coaching Furman, Mildred and a young Somerville rider named Harry Naismith.

Furman Kugler. *Courtesy of Middle Earth, Bridgewater, Tour of Somerville Archives.*

A cycling phenom, Furman Kugler on October 19, 1935, won his first amateur race—a 2.5-mile junior match in Philadelphia. His prizes included a ruby-studded gold medal, a suit of clothes and an overcoat. The *Daily Home News*, a New Brunswick daily afternoon newspaper, reported that, when asked for his reaction to his victory, Furman said: "I'm glad I won… but I'm only half as happy as my daddy."

Furman, born August 29, 1921, won the national junior title in Buffalo in 1937 and three times was the New Jersey state amateur champ. Naismith and Furman entered the sixty-mile Camden to Atlantic City road race, held April 28, 1940, and sponsored by the Italo-American Club of Philadelphia. Fifteen-year-old Naismith finished first with a sixteen-minute handicap, while Furman covered the distance in the fastest time from scratch.

Mildred recalled that, in 1940, while riding home from a competition, she and her brother asked their father: Why do we always have to drive so far to compete in bicycle races? Why can't we race closer to home? "Well, now that's a thought," Mildred said, quoting her father's understated response to the question. After returning to New Jersey, Pop went to work, used his local connections and lined up sponsors for a race in Somerville.

However, the tour nearly was scuttled before it ever started. Czajkowski said when Pop first applied for a permit to stage the race, state officials denied the request, pointing out that racing was prohibited on state roadways (the course included a start-and-finish area on Somerville's Main Street, which is also Route 28, a state road). As a result, Kugler told the lawmakers that the event would be known as a "tour," not a race, and the approval was given.

The first Tour of Somerville was held on May 30, 1940. The criterium attracted a field of 137 riders, including state champs from New England and the Midwest, vying for $1,200 in prizes. Mayor Freas L. Hess fired the starting gun, and at the end of fifty miles, Furman Kugler was the winner of the inaugural race.

The day after the race, Otto W. Eisele, the president of the Amateur Bicycle League of America, drafted a congratulatory letter to Pop Kugler:

> *My dear Fred, I would feel ungrateful indeed if I should let many days go by without writing to thank you, for the record, for the wonderful bike race you put on in Somerville yesterday. You know I have been following them in every part of the country for some 20 years and, in every respect, your race exceeded all others. You should, of course, be proud of your fine son, who rode like the champion he is. And you should also be proud of your townspeople, your club and yourself. You did a great job.*

Later that summer, Pop Kugler packed up his car and drove his daughter, son and Naismith to the national amateur championship races, which were held August 30 to September 2, 1940, at Chandler Park, Detroit. The Somerville trio rode under the colors of the Plainfield Wheelmen. Pop watched with pride as Furman won the senior men's title, Mildred won the senior women's title and Naismith garnered the men's junior title. Furman won the five- and ten-mile matches, Mildred won a five-mile race and Naismith won a ten-mile match and placed fourth in a two-mile race.

The accomplishment was hailed throughout New Jersey and the national press. Prior to going to the national championship in Detroit, the three Somerville riders placed first in their respective categories in the New Jersey amateur road championships.

The second Tour of Somerville was held on May 30, 1941, and Furman again was the winner. The following year, Mildred recalled that Furman had decided to sit it out in order to coach his friend, Carl Anderson of Clifton, who won the tour's 1942 crown.

Mayor Freas Hess lauds Somerville's trio of 1940 national champs during a downtown celebration. Pictured are (from left) Fred Kugler Sr., Pop Kugler, Furman Kugler, Harry Naismith, Mildred Kugler, Mayor Hess and Carl Rauber. *Courtesy of Middle Earth, Bridgewater, Tour of Somerville Archives.*

THE TELEGRAMS

The tour was suspended from 1943 to 1946, due to World War II. In 1945, the Somerville community was shaken by tragic news from the front lines. On August 17, Furman Kugler, serving in the navy, died aboard the USS *Wichita*, near the Pacific island of Okinawa.

"The telegram came to our house. It was very sad," Mildred said. "Pop and Furman were best friends. They loved riding together. My mother, Edna, took it very hard." She said the family decided to have Furman interred at the Punch Bowl National Cemetery in Hawaii, Lot 172. She visited his grave in April 2010. "It was something I always wanted to do; something I felt I had to do."

Anderson, a 1937 graduate of Clifton High School, was born in Sweden and came to the United States with his parents when he was four years old. He joined the army in July 1944 and went overseas in January 1945. Serving in General George S. Patton Jr.'s Third Army, Anderson died in Belgium March 8, 1945, from injuries he had suffered three days earlier. His parents received their telegram on March 17, according to a report in the March 20, 1945 edition of the *Herald News*.

He joined the Triangle Cycling Club of Paterson in 1935 and won the 1941 New Jersey senior amateur championship on July 20 at Brookdale Park, Bloomfield. He was the 1943 all-around national cycling champion. In one of his final races, he placed fifth in a sixty-seven-mile race between Elgin, Illinois, and Chicago, even though he competed with a ninety-minute handicap.

TOUR LUMINARIES

When the tour resumed in 1947, it was renamed the Kugler-Anderson Memorial Tour of Somerville. Donald Sheldon of Nutley won that year and again in 1948. Sheldon, a 1948 graduate of Nutley High School and a member of the Triangle Cycle Club, later became a member of the U.S. Olympic team and competed in the 1952 Games in Helsinki, Finland.

Saling, a protégé of Pop Kugler and a 1958 graduate of Somerville High School, worked at Kugler's bike shop in the mid-1950s. Saling began racing as an amateur in 1956. After serving in the navy, he became associated with the Tour of Somerville, first as a racer and then as the announcer. Today, he is recognized as the familiar "voice" of the tour.

The Tour of Somerville

Vince Menci, an aspiring fourteen-year-old cyclist living in Somerville, was a rider with the Plainfield Wheelmen club and a face in the crowd when Furman Kugler won the first Tour of Somerville. The excitement of the race inspired the young Menci, who quickly persuaded his mother to purchase a Schwinn cycle from Pop's shop.

Before he left for the war, Furman Kugler befriended Menci, and the two would ride together on weeknights throughout the rolling hills of Somerset County. After Furman Kugler went off to war, Menci continued to train under Pop Kugler's guidance and won the New Jersey men's senior division

Don Sheldon of Nutley won the Tour of Somerville in 1947 and 1948. *Courtesy of Middle Earth, Bridgewater, Tour of Somerville Archives.*

title in 1945 at Brookdale Park. He placed fifth in the 1947 tour.

Menci joined the army in 1950 and was deployed to the Korean War as a member of the artillery battery of the Forty-fifth Infantry Division. Returning to Somerville after the war, Menci remained active in the Somerville cycling scene and became an integral part of the tour. He served as the New Jersey district representative of the Amateur Bicycle League of America (which eventually became part of USA Cycling) and was associated with the original U.S. Bicycling Hall of Fame, which was founded in 1986.

The hall of fame established its exhibition space in April 1987 in downtown Somerville. It was housed in a room at the First National Bank of New Jersey, at Main and Bridge Streets. In 2009, the hall announced it was relocating to Davis, California, and held opening ceremonies at the new site on April 24, 2010.

As it has grown throughout the years, the Tour of Somerville—itself inducted into the hall of fame as a cycling institution in 1993—has attracted

In 1951, Pop Kugler led an American amateur cycling team on a month-long tour of Japan. Two years later, he hosted a Japanese cycling team, which competed in the Tour of Somerville and toured North America. *Courtesy of Middle Earth, Bridgewater, Tour of Somerville Archives.*

top international racers from Japan, Russia, Australia, Canada, New Zealand, Mexico, South America and Europe.

Garden State riders have made their mark in the tour over the years. John Chiselko won the tour in 1954 when he was a senior at Somerville High School. A member of the Somerset Wheelmen, Chiselko won state championships during the early 1950s and earned the title of U.S. BAR (Best All Round) champion in 1954.

Jack Heid of Westwood won the tour in 1956. In August 23, 1942, racing as a member of the Harrington Park Sprocketeers, Heid won the New Jersey senior championship at Brookdale Park, capturing the five-mile event and finishing third in the ten-mile match. Heid was a three-time New Jersey amateur senior champ (1942, 1946 and 1947), a member of the 1948 Olympic team and won a bronze medal in the 1949 World Championships. He entered the hall of fame in 1989.

Closter resident Jack Simes III won the tour in 1967 and 1969. Inducted into the hall in 1995, Simes was a member of two Pan American, three Olympic and eight World Champion teams. He garnered silver medals in the 1967 Pan American games and the 1968 World Championships. His

Jack Heid, winner of the 1956 Tour of Somerville. *Courtesy of Jeff Groman, Jazz Sport LLC.*

father, John Weston Simes II—an outstanding cyclist in the 1930s who entered the hall in 1999—served as Jack's coach. Other New Jersey winners include Hugh Starrs, Jonas Carney, J-Me Carney and Lucas Haedo.

The tour has evolved into a full weekend of cycling events, such as the Manville Cycling Madness, the Mildred Kugler Women's Open, the Bound Brook Criterium, the Torpey Memorial Road Race and Menci Criterium. Frank J. Torpey was a committee member of the original hall of fame and served as the group's spokesman.

Mildred Kugler, born September 17, 1924, won three New Jersey women's senior titles, in addition to her 1940 national championship, and retired in 1942. Ten years later, after being married and having four children, she came out of retirement and reclaimed the New Jersey title in 1952 and 1953. In 2002, she was inducted into the U.S. Bicycling Hall of Fame, joining her brother, who was tapped in 1995. Mildred's sister Shirley became New Jersey's state champion in 1954, with her other sister, Anna, finishing in second place.

The Mildred Kugler Women's Open, launched in 1967, has established itself as a premier U.S. event, with top riders like Karen Strong and Sue Novara-Reber dominating in the early years as consecutive three-time repeat winners. Laura Van Gilder, who grew up in the Pocono Mountain region of Pennsylvania, also has won the open three times (1999, 2002 and 2005).

"I've been embraced by the people of Somerville like a hometown girl. Somerville is like a big family event," Van Gilder said, explaining the "family" dynamic stems from the hospitality of tour organizers and the bonds that form among competitive athletes. "There's a lot of sacrifice that goes with being a cyclist. You spend time training and traveling to races. Everyone is after the same prize and everyone is enduring the same elements. You develop camaraderie with your competitors. Once you understand what it's all about, you feel very welcomed on the racing circuit."

Dottie Saling (married to Joe Saling) was inducted into the hall of fame in 2010 as a "contributor" to the sport, honored for her fifty-plus years in cycling. She was a member of the USA Cycling's board of directors and became the first female vice-president. She also served on committees for the Pan American and Olympic games.

"The First Coach"

Dottie and Joe Saling bought Pop Kugler's bicycle shop in 1967. The new owners relocated the shop to South Bridge Street and sold the business in 1981. Pop retired to Margate, Florida but visited Somerville often to be part of the tour festivities. The Somerville Area Jaycees, in cooperation with the Somerset Wheelmen, took over the operations of the Tour of Somerville.

Pop celebrated his fiftieth birthday by riding solo on the fifty-mile tour course and did it again on his sixtieth birthday. Honoring his lifetime contributions to the sport, Pop Kugler, in 1987, was tapped as the first inductee of the U.S. Bicycling Hall of Fame. He died October 24, 1991, in Winter Garden, Florida.

"He was the first coach most of us had," Joe Saling said, referring to Somerville-area cyclists, quoted in an article by the *Courier-News*. "He was like a second father. I was very fortunate. I had a great dad, but I also had Pop. He taught me a lot."

Tour of Somerville, circa 1950. *Courtesy of Middle Earth, Bridgewater, Tour of Somerville Archives.*

Saling said Pop Kugler was well aware of his place in cycling history. "He had an appreciation for all the things he was able to accomplish," Saling said. "He felt good about his legacy."

He also had a wry sense of humor. "Pop was the National Professional Tandem Champion (in 1936 with Russell Allen) and this event was never held again," Saling said. As a result, Pop Kugler maintained his claim to fame was that he always would be the undefeated U.S. tandem champ.

The Tour of Somerville is the oldest, continuously operated amateur cycling race in the United States. The course is a flat, four-turn, 1.2-mile-per-lap circuit through Somerville's downtown, which annually attracts crowds of up to twenty thousand. Middle Earth, a nonprofit community outreach agency that serves teenagers and young adults in Somerset County, which was a sponsor of the Tour of Somerville for over thirty years, became the sole operator of the event in 1997. The tour will mark its sixty-eighth year in 2011.

EPILOGUE

Vince Menci attended a cycling banquet in Newark with Pop Kugler in the mid-1940s. The affair was organized by cycling's "other" Pop—John Pop Brennan, the master bicycle builder of Newark—as a way to honor the great bike riders of the day. "While we were at the banquet, Pop (Kugler) introduced me to Frank Kramer," Menci said. "I shook his hand, but I was young and had no idea who he was."

Decades later, that handshake would provide a spiritual connection for Menci. Not long after the original U.S. Bicycling Hall of Fame was established in Somerville, it featured a special display of Frank Kramer memorabilia, which was donated by Gordon Wright. Kramer was Wright's great-great uncle. While attending the exhibition, Wright introduced himself to Menci. The two began to chat, and Menci recounted the experience of meeting Frank Kramer years ago at the Newark banquet.

Wright lingered in the hall of fame that day, spending more than an hour silently observing the various photos and artifacts of the great champion who once dominated the Newark Velodrome. Menci quietly observed him and realized that being at the exhibit was a profound emotional experience for Wright.

Before taking his leave, Wright approached Menci. He shook his hand and said: "Vince, I've got to tell you—I didn't expect to stay here this long, but I feel my uncle's presence here today." As Wright walked out the door, Menci smiled and felt a chill. "That was my greatest experience in all my years in cycling."

May the wheels keep turning. May the ride never end.

BIBLIOGRAPHY

NEWSPAPERS AND MAGAZINES

American Motorcyclist and Bicyclist (AM&B)
Atlantic City Daily Press
Atlantic City Evening Union
Courier-News
Daily Princetonian
Herald News
Los Angeles Times
Mount Holly Herald
New York Times
Newark Call
Newark Evening News
Nutley Sun
Orange Chronicle
Orange Journal
Outing Magazine
Passaic Daily News
Plainfield Daily Press
Rutgers Targum
Somerset Messenger
Star-Ledger
Time

BIBLIOGRAPHY

Articles

Nye, Peter. "Bill Honeman Inspired the Original Stars and Stripes Jersey." Classic Cycles.com, www.classiccycleus.com.

———. "Newark, N.J., Started a National Cycling Tradition." U.S. Bicycling Hall of Fame, http://www.usbhof.com.

———. "Victor Hopkins: Early Olympian Pedals from Hometown to Olympic Trials." *Cycling USA* 15, no. 5 (May 1992).

BOOKS AND PROGRAMS

Associated Cycling Club (ACC) of Philadelphia. "Official Catalogue and Souvenir of the ACC Cycle Show," February 15–22, 1892. Industrial Hall, Philadelphia, PA.

Gabriele, Michael C. *The Nutley Velodrome.* Self published, 1983.

Harper, Ted. *Six Days of Madness.* Stroud, Ontario: Pacesetter Press, 1993.

League of American Wheelmen, "14th Annual Meet, League of American Wheelman, World's Fair Cycling Tournament," August 5–12, 1893. Chicago, IL.

Motorcycling and Bicycling. Chicago, IL: Tradepress Publishing Corp., 1919.

Nye, Peter J. *Hearts of Lions: The History of American Bicycle Racing.* New York: W.W. Norton & Co., 1988.

Nye, Peter J., Jeff Groman and Mark Tyson. *The Six-Day Bicycle Races: America's Jazz-Age Sport.* San Francisco, CA: Van de Plas Publications/ Cycling Publishing, 2006.

"Official Program, Fifty-Fifth International 6-Day Bicycle Race," November 26–December 2, 1933. Madison Square Garden, New York, NY.

Palmer, Arthur Judson. *Riding High: The Story of the Bicycle.* New York: E.P. Dutton & Co. Inc., 1956.

Pratt, Charles E. *The American Bicycler.* Cambridge and Boston, MA: Riverside Press, 1879.

Presbrey, Frank, and James Hugh Moffatt. *Athletics at Princeton: A History.* New York: Frank Presbrey Co., 1901.

Ricord, F.W., ed. *The History of Union County, New Jersey.* Newark, NJ: East Jersey History Company, 1897. Reprinted online, Bowie, MD: Heritage Books Inc., 2001.

The World Almanac of Book of Facts. New York: Press Publishing Co, 1902.

HISTORICAL SOCIETIES, ORGANIZATIONS, LIBRARIES AND OTHER SOURCES

Atlantic City Free Public Library. Atlantic City, New Jersey.
Burlington County Library. Burlington County, New Jersey.
Clifton Main Memorial Library. Clifton, New Jersey.
Fawkner Crematorium and Memorial Park. Fawkner, Victoria, Australia.
H.B. Smith Industrial Village Conservancy. Burlington County, New Jersey.
League of American Bicyclists. Washington, D.C.
Metz Bicycle Museum. Freehold, New Jersey.
Middle Earth. Bridgewater, New Jersey.
Millburn Free Public Library. Millburn, New Jersey.
Newark Public Library. Newark, New Jersey.
The Nutley Historical Society. Nutley, New Jersey.
Nutley Public Library. Nutley New Jersey.
Old Stone House of Brooklyn. Brooklyn, New York.
Orange Public Library. Orange, New Jersey.
Plainfield Public Library, Plainfield, New Jersey.
Princeton University Library. Princeton, New Jersey.
Rutgers University Libraries. New Brunswick, New Jersey.
Somerset County Libraries. Somerset County, New Jersey
Trenton Historical Society. Trenton Public Library, Trenton, New Jersey.
USA Cycling. Colorado Springs, Colorado.
The U.S. Bicycling Hall of Fame, Davis, California.

ONLINE RESOURCES

A.G. Lichtenstein & Associates Inc. "The New Jersey Historic Bridge Survey, September 1994." New Jersey Department of Transportation. http://www.state.nj.us/transportation/works/environment/pdf/Survey_Doc.pdf.
"Arthur A. Zimmerman." DVRBS.com, http://www.dvrbs.com/people/camdenpeople-AAZimmerman.htm.
Australian Dictionary of Biography, http://adbonline.anu.edu.au.
Baird, Christine V. "Neighborhood Snapshot: Waverly," April 10, 2008. NJ.com, http://www.nj.com/newark/index.ssf/2008/04/neighborhood_snapshot_waverly.html.
Bikeraceinfo.com.

California Bicycle Museum (part of the U.S. Bicycling Hall of Fame), http://www.usbhof.org/.

Canada's Sports Hall of Fame, http://www.sportshall.ca.

Dorfman, Sid. "Cycling Flourished in Newark," August 9, 2008. NJ.com, http://www.nj.com/newark/index.ssf/2008/08/cycling_flourished_in_newark.html.

"1888 Interview with Fred Wood." Hilldodger's Cycling History Site, http://cyclinghistory.blogspot.com.

Famous Birthdays for October 13," HistoryOrb.com, http://www.historyorb.com/birthdays/october/13.

"Franco Giorgetti." SR/Olympic Sports, http://www.sports-reference.com/olympics/athletes/gi/franco-giorgetti-1.html.

Free Library of Philadelphia, http://www.freelibrary.org.

Iowa Soldier's Orphans' Home, http://blogs.davenportlibrary.com/sc/?tag=iowa-soldiers-orphans-home.

Major Taylor Association Inc., http://www.majortaylorassociation.org.

The Major Taylor Society, http://www.majortaylor.com.

McNeil, Wilbur. "Weequahic Park." Project for Public Spaces, www.pps.org/great_public_spaces.

Monmouth County Historical Association, http://www.monmouthhistory.org.

Old Newark Memories, http://www.oldnewark.com.

"Olympics at Sports-Reference.com," http://www.sports-reference.com.

Six-Day Racing, http://www.6dayracing.ca.

Sport Australia Hall of Fame, http://www.sahof.org.au/hallof fame.

The-Sports.org/cycling.

Statnekov, Daniel K. Chapter 5 of "Pioneers of American Motorcycle Racing." Statnekov.com, http://www.statnekov.com/motorcycles/lives5.html.

"Weequahic Park." Essex County Parks, http://www.essex-countynj.org.

———. Newarkology, http://www.newarkhistory.com/weequahicpark.html.

ABOUT THE AUTHOR

A lifelong New Jersey resident and a 1975 graduate of Montclair State University, Michael C. Gabriele has worked as a journalist at various newspapers and magazines in the metropolitan area for over thirty years. He is a member of the Nutley Historical Society and the Passaic County Historical Society. Born in Passaic, he grew up in Nutley and currently resides in Clifton with his family.

Courtesy of Melissa McNally.

Visit us at
www.historypress.net